D1542101

THE BOSTON MARATHON BOMBING

THE LONG RUN FROM TERROR TO RENEWAL

By The Associated Press

Mango Media
Miami
in collaboration with
The Associated Press

 AP EDITIONS

AP Editions

Copyright © 2015 Associated Press. All rights reserved. This material may not be published, broadcast, rewritten or redistributed.

Published by Mango Media, Inc.

www.mangomedia.us

No part of this publication may be reproduced, distributed or transmitted in any form or by any means, without prior written permission.

This is a work of non-fiction adapted from articles and content by journalists of The Associated Press and published with permission.

The Boston Marathon Bombing: The Long Run from Terror to Renewal

ISBN: 978-1-63353-261-8

Cover Photo:

Medical workers aid injured people at the finish line of the 2013 Boston Marathon following an explosion in Boston, April 15, 2013. (AP Photo/Charles Krupa)

Publisher's Note

AP Editions brings together stories and photographs by the professional journalists of The Associated Press.

These stories are presented in their original form and are intended to provide a snapshot of history as the moments occurred.

We hope you enjoy these selections from the front lines of newsgathering.

"I went into the shower laughing, so happy about what this day was all about and I came out and it was all over. It's just that sense of completely feeling just vulnerable, like something's been taken from us for no reason, for absolutely no reason, and it's just completely senseless."

-- Meredith Saillant, Boston Marathon runner, April 15, 2013

TABLE OF CONTENTS

THE LONGEST MARATHON

Associated Press photographer Charlie Krupa had set himself up amid the celebrative crowd and snapped their triumphant pictures from a makeshift overhead bridge.

After covering 25 Boston Marathons, he knew the drill. He then hustled to the press area to edit these photos and transmit them to the world so he could hurry back to capture the unpredictable but always memorable next part of this carefree rite of spring. What would those follow-up images show this year? Would it be the runner kneeling to propose to his girlfriend at the finish line? Or maybe an exhausted participant struggling, even crawling, across? Would it be someone clowning, arms outstretched, swooping and dipping like a stunt plane, or, as happened one year, someone completing the race by walking on his hands?

Who knew what was ahead on this festive Patriots' Day when, as usual, state workers and schoolchildren got their mid-April Monday off and hundreds of thousands of others played hooky to descend en masse on the city for the quintessentially Bostonian celebration of the end of another long New England winter? The holiday is a chance to see the Red Sox play one of their first home games of the new season at Fenway Park. A chance to lick the year's first ice cream cone or slyly sip from a beer concealed in a koozie or a cooler. A chance to light a grill and lounge in a lawn chair.

Maybe best of all, a chance to cheer on the day's signature event: that sweaty stream of jubilant, jostling humanity known as the Boston Marathon.

On the cool, bright afternoon of April 15, 2013, near the marathon's blue-and-yellow finish line decal on Boylston Street, slowly sunburning spectators were clapping and clanging cowbells for the stream of 27,000 runners. Each was someone's friend or spouse or significant other, parent, child, colleague or neighbor. Each was taking part for a reason: to set a personal best, to raise money for charity, or simply to experience, for the first time or the tenth, the magic of America's most venerable footrace.

Rita Jeptoo, of Kenya, left, and Lelisa Desisa, of Ethiopia, right, pose for photographers after winning the women's and men's division of the 2013 running of the Boston Marathon, April 15, 2013. (AP Photo/Charles Krupa)

At 2:49 p.m., when the first deep boom sounded amid the happy din, it didn't immediately register to most people. They heard it, but to some, it sounded like the celebratory cannon fire that rings out over the Charles River every Fourth of July when the Boston Pops orchestra plays the "1812 Overture" outdoors. Others initially thought it was a transformer explosion or a manhole cover blown into the air by a buildup of subterranean steam. Something urban. Something innocuous. Nothing sinister.

Krupa was filing pictures when he heard it. He was in the press room set up at the Fairmont Copley Plaza Hotel. That, he thought, must be a heavy piece of equipment falling. Or maybe the bone-shaking thud a giant steel trash bin makes when the garbage truck emptying it drops it back on the street. But 12 seconds later, there was another explosion. Indoors, Krupa couldn't hear the cheering turn to screaming, couldn't smell the stench of sulfurous smoke and burnt hair, couldn't see the people collapsed on the sidewalk or the spectators knocking over barricades in their rush to get away from Boylston. Seconds before, it had had the atmosphere of a party. Now, it was strewn with limbs and spattered with blood.

Still, Krupa knew something was seriously wrong. As he scanned the press room, searching for clues to what was happening, someone suddenly entered and announced that no one could leave.

"We're in lockdown," the official said, as security guards took up posts at both main doors to prevent anyone from coming or going.

Then Krupa remembered: Behind the drapes near a podium was a door that led to another door to get out of the building. Before anyone could stop him, the 28-year AP veteran photographer grabbed three cameras, a laptop computer and a wireless transmitting device and ducked behind the drapes. By the time he got to the outside door, three guards were approaching it. He slipped by before they could lock it. Krupa, a runner who usually logged about 25 miles each week, sprinted from the hotel, crossing Copley Square and onto Boylston Street.

At the medical tent, it was too soon after the explosions; there was no real activity yet. The scene was eerily quiet: "There was really no sound. No sirens or anything."

He moved on. He could see a lot of commotion down the street, then focused on a man in a cowboy hat about a half-block away, helping someone in a wheelchair. The man in the hat would turn out to be Carlos Arredondo, a spectator who leaped in to assist, holding a tourniquet on the right leg of the stricken man, Jeff Bauman. An EMT was applying pressure to the same leg, and a medical volunteer was pushing the wheelchair.

As Krupa got closer, he saw the extent of the injuries as Bauman's eyes locked on his: "His face was ashen. There was no color in his face. And as I got closer, I could see how shattered he was, that he had no legs, that these three people that were with him, they were going to get him the care he needed."

He started taking pictures, running alongside as the rescuers rushed Bauman to an ambulance. One of the photos would become an iconic image of the bombings' horror.

He kept running, knowing he needed to get past the finish line, where he could see people hunched over the injured. Stopped from passing under the photo bridge by a Boston police officer, he climbed back up to try to get overview shots. The scene was ghastly.

"EMTs. Firefighters. Everybody was triaging all these people in a cluster," he said. Medical attendants and volunteers worked frantically, using their own belts and shoelaces as tourniquets.

"They were attending to people, getting them on stretchers and getting them off Boylston Street. It was like watching ants. Everyone knew what job they had to do." Something else registered through his lens: Although the panicked were peeling away in every direction, a quarter of the crowd was running toward the blast sites to help.

Medical workers aid injured people at the finish line of the 2013 Boston Marathon, April 15, 2013. (AP Photo/Charles Krupa)

Three people lay dead or dying -- two women in their 20s and an 8-year-old boy. More than 260 others were wounded, scores of them moaning and dabbing at bleeding gashes. Sixteen clutched helplessly at legs that dangled from shreds of tissue or were simply gone; another had her mangled leg amputated months later.

This carnage was wrought, as the city and the world would learn, by the jagged shrapnel unleashed by twin pressure-cooker bombs. On Patriots' Day, commemorating the first battles of the Revolutionary War, terrorists had struck at Boston's heart.

Boston, of course, is a city acclaimed for its world-class health care, with multiple trauma centers with vast experience lying within a mile of the bombing scene. Fifteen minutes after the blasts, Krupa recalls, no one was left on the street -- every victim had been rushed to a hospital. And even with the many ghastly injuries, nearly everyone hurt survived.

Tragically, nothing could be done to save the lives of three who died within moments of the explosions: Lingzi Lu, a 23-year-old Boston University graduate student from China; Krystle Campbell, a 29-year-old restaurant manager from suburban Medford, Massachusetts; and Martin Richard, an 8-year-old boy from Boston's Dorchester neighborhood who was watching the marathon with his family.

Still on the chaotic streets, Krupa kept snapping scenes, which he likened to war-torn Sarajevo, and operated on adrenalin and instinct. "There's no manual that says when a bomb goes off in your city, this is what you've got to do," he said. He detached, intuitively understanding that what was unfolding before him was transcendent. "My responsibility is to document what happens in front of me."

In that first frantic hour, as people raced for reassurance that their loved ones were OK, Boston's cell phone and wireless networks were overwhelmed. Krupa still tears up when he recalls how his panicked teenage son and daughter had texted him; he responded that he was fine, busy, but not in any danger -- don't worry. He paused a moment to text his wife: "I'm OK. Tell my Mom and Dad I'm OK."

Back at the press center, word spread that a little boy was among the dead. AP Sports Writer Jimmy Golen vividly remembers that moment:

"I got up to walk it off. In the bathroom, a Boston police officer was at the mirror, wiping the tears from his reddened eyes. I patted him on the back but said nothing."

Fear gripped the city. With the bomber -- or bombers? -- still on the loose, a no-fly zone was imposed over downtown Boston. The Bruins and Celtics canceled games.

Shortly after 6 p.m., President Barack Obama addressed the nation: "We will find out who did this. We'll find out why they did this. Any responsible individuals, any responsible groups, will feel the full weight of justice."

Authorities asked the public to submit any photos or video they took at the marathon and tips they had about anything suspicious they saw. Local, state and federal agents began gathering thousands of pieces of evidence and combing the massive crime scene for clues. The FBI collected surveillance videos from businesses lining Boylston Street.

Investigators found nails, ball bearings and other shrapnel everywhere, even on the rooftop of a four-story hotel. They also found pieces of pressure cookers and the tattered remains of two black backpacks used to carry the bombs.

Fellow AP Boston photographer Elise Amendola, in search of a high vantage point, rode the elevator to the top floor of the Westin Hotel and found it occupied by law enforcement. She went down a floor and started knocking on doors. A couple let her into their room so she could make some pictures from the window of the scene on Boylston below.

Krupa remembers the next 100 hours like this: "On Monday, the city was shattered physically. And as the week went on, there was a sort of shattering emotionally." On Tuesday, restless, he rose at dawn and made a photo of a solitary runner in silhouette moving along the Charles River. It was a picture that seemed to carry an unwritten message: Even though everything instantly had changed, what makes Boston what it is endured; the city would survive this.

A solitary runner heads down the bank of the Charles River in Cambridge, Mass. at dawn, April 16, 2013. (AP Photo/Charles Krupa)

Rumors swirled and misinformation circulated among rival state and federal law enforcement agencies, some of it leaking to reporters. At one point, several news organizations, including AP, reported that a suspect was in custody. It was based on information from insistent authorities, but it was wrong.

Billy Evans, Boston's elfin, high-energy police superintendent who later would ascend to the top job of commissioner, had run the marathon for the 18th time Monday and was soaking his aching muscles in a hot tub afterward when he heard about the explosions. At first, he didn't believe it was terrorism -- maybe a transformer fire, he thought. The city had had a few of those over the past couple of years. Reality sank in when he got to Boylston.

"I remember looking at the tragic scene and the destruction and thinking about how an hour before, I had run down the street, and how much joy and excitement there was," he said. "To see the bodies lying in front of the Forum and the banners blown apart: It was a vision I don't think I'll ever get out of my head."

The rest of the week was a frenzied blur for him: setting up officers to protect a 20-block area, searching for the bombers, planning security for an Obama visit. By Wednesday, Evans was told the FBI thought they had spotted the bombers on surveillance video walking down Boylston and standing amid the crowds, each carrying a backpack. They still didn't know who they were.

On Thursday, three days after the bombings, the FBI called a news conference to release photos and surveillance video of two men, their names still unknown. (It would be Friday before authorities identified the men they were hunting: brothers Tamerlan and Dzhokhar Tsarnaev.)

For now, suspect No. 1 was simply called "Black Hat." Suspect No. 2 was "White Hat." Grainy images showed them nonchalantly mingling with the crowd packing Boylston's sidewalks.

Their pictures were transmitted everywhere, and the manhunt intensified. It didn't take long to flush them out.

Within hours, a frantic emergency call came in to police: At the Massachusetts Institute of Technology, a campus police officer had been shot to death. He would be identified as 26-year-old Sean Collier.

Soon afterward, a terrified carjack victim told authorities he had just escaped from two men. One of them claimed he had bombed the Boston Marathon and had just killed a police officer in Cambridge.

Police spotted the stolen Mercedes SUV in Watertown. A firefight erupted after two men started shooting and hurling explosives at police, including pipe bombs and a pressure-cooker bomb like the ones used at the marathon.

A Watertown police officer later would testify that Tamerlan Tsarnaev emptied his gun, then threw it at him. Dzhokhar, behind

the wheel of the stolen Mercedes, then drove straight at three officers who were trying to handcuff Tamerlan on the ground. Dzhokhar
ran over his brother, dragging him down the street. Tamerlan died
of gunshot wounds and injuries from being struck by the car.

But Dzhokhar escaped -- simply vanished -- managing to
elude a massive police dragnet that gave normally carefree, colle-
giate Boston and its leafy environs a surreal quality in scenes
broadcast live around the country and the world.

Armored vehicles rolled down the streets of Watertown, while
police and SWAT teams conducted door-to-door searches. In an unprecedented announcement, Gov. Deval Patrick issued a "shelter-
in-place" order for Boston and surrounding communities, instruct-
ing people to stay in their homes as the search continued.

Police in tactical gear arrive on an armored police vehicle as they surround an apartment
building while looking for a suspect in Watertown, April 19, 2013. (AP Photo/Charles
Krupa)

Typically busy streets were deserted, schools were closed and
fretful parents kept their children indoors. The pulse of a major
American city weirdly flatlined for hours as people watched and
waited. It had been Monday when the bombers struck; now it was
Friday, and one of them was still out there, somewhere.

Jesse Bonelli, a young video game artist living in locked-down Watertown, dutifully stayed inside his apartment. But just in case, he removed a decorative machete from a wall and sharpened it, explaining, "It's the only weapon I have. I want to be ready in case anyone bursts into the house."

After everything that had happened, he said, "I keep wondering what's next."

Krupa remembers Watertown as a "Wild West" place, militarized by gun-slinging good guys. "It was seriously crazy to be sitting in my car filing pictures and looking in my rear view mirror and seeing two tanks and 100 guys in SWAT gear."

All day, the drama kept the nation transfixed, and locals on edge. Finally, around 6 p.m., the governor and other officials announced the lifting of the shelter-in-place order, even though Tsarnaev hadn't yet been found.

When David Hennebrry ventured outside his home on a quiet Watertown street, he noticed something amiss. The shrink wrap on his boat appeared loose. When he peered inside, he saw blood -- then a man lying on his side.

Billy Evans was the incident commander for Boston police at the Watertown search scene. After the lockdown ended and people emerged from their houses, he said, some of the hundreds of police officers started to leave, but his officers wanted to keep looking.

"When I asked my captain, he said, 'Boss, give us 15 minutes, we have about five more blocks to search,'" Evans said. "Fifteen minutes go by, and he said: 'Give me five more minutes.'"

Just then, Evans got word about the man in the boat. He and two officers raced to the scene in his unmarked Ford Fusion. When he got there, he noticed something poking through the tarp over the boat, "almost like he had a gun poking at it."

He called for tactical backup, to prepare to get the man out of the boat. "The problem at that time is everyone had been searching for him for a long time. They had adrenalin pumping. People were coming from all directions. For whatever reason, someone let off a round. Once one let off a round, we had multiple shots fired," Evans said.

"I was screaming," he recalled in his thick Boston accent, "'Hold yah FI-YAH! Hold yah FI-YAH!'"

Within 20 seconds or so, the shots stopped. An FBI hostage rescue team used flash grenades to try to flush Tsarnaev out of the boat. After agents ordered him to come out with his hands up, he sat up, then climbed out of the boat, covered with blood.

Just before 9 p.m., Boston police sent a triumphant tweet: "CAPTURED!!! The hunt is over. The search is done. The terror is over. And justice has won. Suspect in custody."

Celebrations erupted in and around Boston. Chants of "USA! USA!" went up as people poured back into the streets after five days of fear. Residents of Watertown cheered and thanked police as Tsarnaev was taken away in an ambulance.

"I will always remember the feeling leaving Watertown. People were out waving flags, people were clapping like we had just won the war," recalled Evans. "College kids were coming out of their dorms. They were marching in the street. For the week we went through, it was quite emotional for all of us."

The next day, star Red Sox slugger David Ortiz gave an emotional speech thanking police for capturing Tsarnaev. "This is our f-----g city!" Big Papi said to loud cheers from the crowd at Fenway Park.

Evans said he and others who'd been on the front lines felt the same way: "All of us took personally that they blew up our marathon and they blew up our city. At Fenway, when they played the national anthem, I remember saluting the flag and I remember being teary-eyed."

Within 24 hours of when the FBI had released the images of the bombing suspects -- which were spread around the world on social media -- the agency was flooded with 10,000 online tips and thousands of phone calls. And yet it was not a tipster who had managed to positively identify the suspects.

That fell to the feds' high-tech crimefighting tools. After Tamerlan was pronounced dead, FBI agents scanned the prints on his cold fingertips using Quick Capture, portable technology designed to run instant background checks. Tamerlan's ID led to a records check on family members -- and up popped Dzhokhar's driver's license photo.

But who were these two brothers. And why had they done this?

The Tsarnaev family moved to the U.S. from Russia in 2002, settling in Cambridge. They were ethnic Chechens who had lived in the former Soviet republic of Kyrgyzstan and the Dagestan region of Russia, an area bordering Chechnya that has been plagued by Islamic insurgency and tensions between ethnic groups.

Parents Anzor and Zubeidat and their four children -- Tamerlan, Dzhokhar, Bella and Ailina -- appeared to adjust to their new country. Anzor worked as a car mechanic, and the children attended Cambridge schools.

Boston Police Superintendent William Evans speaks during a news conference in Boston as he describes the scene in Watertown, Mass., where Boston Marathon bombing suspect Dzhokhar Tsarnaev was captured hiding in a backyard boat, April 23, 2013. (AP Photo/Elise Amendola)

When Dzhokhar graduated from Cambridge Rindge and Latin School in 2011, he won a $2,500 scholarship and attended the University of Massachusetts-Dartmouth. Tamerlan had some success as an amateur boxer, married an American woman and had a daughter with her.

But more than two years before the bombings, Tamerlan had been placed on U.S. authorities' radar. In March 2011, the Russian intelligence security service FSB told the FBI that Tamerlan was a follower of radical Islam. The FBI opened an investigation, but closed it after finding nothing to link Tamerlan to terrorism.

He went on to spend six months in Dagestan and Chechnya in 2012; his parents had divorced and returned to their homeland by then.

His father told AP reporter Arsen Mollayev in Makhachkala, the capital of Dagestan, that Tamerlan spent most of his time lounging around. "He slept until 3 p.m., and you know, I would ask him: `Have you come here to sleep?' He used to go visiting, here and there. He would go to eat somewhere. Then he would come back and go to bed."

Father and son also visited Chechnya twice together during that period "to see my uncles and aunts. I have lots of them," Anzor Tsarnaev said. He said his son didn't want to leave and had thoughts on how he could go into business. But the father said he encouraged him to go back to the U.S. and try to get citizenship, and Tamerlan returned to the U.S. that July.

But his cousin, Magomed Kartashov, said Tamerlan told him he went to Russia to try to join jihadi fighters. Kartashov told the FBI two months after the marathon bombing that Tamerlan had asked if he had any connections to "people in the forest," referring to jihadis.

In November 2012, he interrupted a sermon at the Islamic Society of Boston Cultural Center about it being acceptable for Muslims to celebrate American holidays. Two months later, he had a second outburst after a sermon that included praise for the Rev. Martin Luther King, Jr.

"Boston Strong." The phrase may have been heard before the bombings, but afterward it became a signature, a slogan capturing the resilience and spirit of survivors and the city itself. It appeared as a Twitter hashtag, on T-shirts, on Fenway's Green Monster wall and on the helmets of the Boston Bruins.

Survivors of the bombing seemed to personify "Boston Strong" _ their slow, painful, determined recoveries covered extensively in news stories.

Former AP reporter Bridget Murphy was thrown into the role of chronicling them after being assigned to cover the survivors of another tragedy. Murphy was supposed to write about the dedication of the marathon's 26-mile marker to the 26 students and educators killed in the Sandy Hook Elementary School shooting in Newtown, Connecticut, just four months earlier. Race day had begun with a symbolic 26 seconds of silence to honor those who died.

Newtown families were running the marathon, and others were there waving signs to show support for the runners. A little girl who was at the school at the time of the December 2012 massacre handed Murphy a Sandy Hook memorial bracelet.

"The reason her family was there was to have a positive experience in the crowd and to have a celebration of sorts," Murphy said. "You could never imagine a few hours later that something like this would happen."

In the months that followed, she and Krupa spent hours at Spaulding Rehabilitation Hospital watching amputees get ready for their first prosthetic limbs. Day after day, they'd go to Spaulding to meet with survivors and witness and chronicle their recovery.

"I felt like they were giving us a gift by letting us be there while they were vulnerable," Murphy said. "A lot of them were very buoyant at the beginning. But as time went on and they were confronted with the reality of what their lives would be like from here on out, a lot of them got frustrated."

"It was very sad. People were struck with some harsh realities," said Murphy, now a reporter with Newsday.

Mery Daniel was one of them. Daniel, a 31-year-old medical school graduate, was near Marathon Sports when the first bomb exploded. Doctors amputated her left leg above the knee.

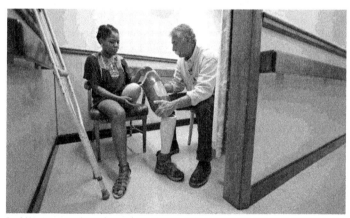

Paul Martino, president of United Prosthetics, talks with Boston Marathon bombing survivor Mery Daniel, left, while helping her try on her newly-built leg at the family-owned company in the Dorchester neighborhood of Boston, June 26, 2013. (AP Photo/Charles Krupa)

Murphy was there when prosthetic specialist Paul Martino helped Daniel slide into the kind of socket that would encase the top of her left leg and connect it to a replacement knee and foot. The fit was awkward initially. Daniel cringed in pain. She tried on two different knees, but even the most advanced technology was clumsy compared with the leg she lost.

"I had one that worked perfectly," she told Martino.

"Yeah," he said. "You did."

As the bombing anniversary approached, so, too, did the 2014 Boston Marathon: the first running of the race since the attacks.

There was never any question that the show would go on. The day after the bombings, the Boston Athletic Association, which organizes the marathon, vowed that the race first staged in 1897 would return. But there were serious security considerations, along with questions of taste (should the race be a solemn commemoration or the usual raucous celebration?) and logistics (should the size of the field be smaller to make the event safer, or larger to accommodate the huge worldwide spike in interest?).

First things first, the organizers decided: They invited the 5,633 runners who were stopped on the second half of the course when the 2013 race was shut down to return and run again. So loud and insistent was the clamor to participate, the B.A.A. gave bibs to 500 others who wrote moving essays explaining their visceral need to run. "Running the 2014 Boston Marathon will help me heal my mind," said Kate Plourd, among those to get a coveted race number.

But before the 2014 edition could be run, 2013 needed to be reckoned with and remembered. Survivors, first responders and family members of those killed came together to mark the anniversary.

A mountain of running shoes, medals, plush toys, notes and other items laid in remembrance at the finish line went on poignant public display. Silent tributes were held from the Statehouse to the White House, where Obama said the 2014 marathon would "show the world the meaning of Boston Strong as a city chooses to run again."

Vice President Joe Biden, in Boston for the anniversary, summed up the mood: "We are Boston. We are America. We respond. We endure. We overcome. And we own the finish line."

In the end, the 2014 field swelled to 35,671 -- the second-largest in race history -- in a powerful show of defiance 12 months after blood stained Boylston Street.

Security was unprecedented: Jets flew low sorties over all eight cities and towns along the route; police snipers took up positions on rooftops; officers with bomb-sniffing dogs fanned out along the course; and a battery of more than 100 surveillance cameras silently scanned the crowds for any signs of trouble. All told, more than 3,500 police -- twice the usual number -- deployed along the course.

Boston Marathon bombing survivor Heather Abbott carries a symbolic torch as she crosses the marathon finish line in Boston, April 13, 2014. (AP Photo/Michael Dwyer)

Meb Keflezighi, a naturalized emigrant from Eritrea, became the first American in 31 years to win the men's race. The four corners of his bib number bore the hand-written names of the three spectators killed by the bombs and the MIT police officer slain during the manhunt. The crowd roared as he approached the finish.

But the loudest cheers of the day came after a moment of silence held at the finish line at 2:49 p.m., the time of the first explosion. The hush that fell over the crowd gave way to boisterous whooping, clapping and the clanging of cowbells.

A banner on one building read: "You are Boston Strong. You Earned This." Even more touching, the thick crowds at the finish line included several bombing survivors. Among them was Heather Abbott, who lost her left leg. Now fitted with an artificial limb, she ran the last half-mile with a friend.

Bill Kole, AP's New England news editor and a veteran of 17 marathons, ran his third Boston with an iPhone to capture 2014's triumphant atmosphere in a series of live tweets: one for every mile of the race. Using the hashtag #26Tweets2Boston, Kole relayed his own thoughts and observations as well as those of fellow runners and spectators -- all determined to recapture the event's joy and whimsy.

At the starting line: "The gun booms, the runners roar; we're off. I'm bobbing in a sea of fist pumps and high fives. Boston's back."

Near the halfway mark: "'I am not in danger. I AM the danger.' T-shirt worn by runner Jenny Welch of Los Angeles."

At the finish line: "Everyone's screaming on Boylston Street. For all the right reasons. 36,000 sweaty, tearful, exuberant reasons."

Once again, Charlie Krupa was back on the footbridge to photograph the race, and he couldn't help but marvel at the euphoria: "The race became whole again."

Dzhokhar Tsarnaev's trial began with a bombshell.

"It was him," lead defense lawyer Judy Clarke acknowledged in her opening statement, startling many in the courtroom by bluntly admitting he participated in the bombings. But Clarke had a bigger point to make: Tamerlan, she insisted, was the mastermind. If not for the radicalized elder brother, she said, the attacks wouldn't have happened.

In the weeks that followed, the jury heard gut-wrenching testimony as survivors took the stand in rapid succession.

Rebekah Gregory was one of the first to tell her story. A young, slender woman with long blond hair, Gregory walked slowly to the witness stand on an artificial limb. Her left leg was ravaged in the bombing, but she fought through 17 surgeries and 19 months to keep it, until the pain was too constant and too debilitating. She finally told doctors to amputate in November 2014, just four months before she would face Tsarnaev.

Sitting in the witness box about 10 feet from the man who maimed her, Gregory described watching the race with her boyfriend and his family. They'd gone to see her boyfriend's mother run. Gregory brought her 5-year-old son, Noah. They were all having fun, soaking in the festive atmosphere, enjoying being part of a Boston institution.

The next thing Gregory remembered was being thrown back and hoisted into the air.

"My first instinct as a mother was, where in the world was my baby, where was my son?" she recalled. She looked down at her leg and saw bones lying next to her on the sidewalk. "Blood was everywhere," she said.

As her eyes searched frantically for her son, she saw a young woman dying on the pavement. She didn't know the woman's name at the time. She later learned it was Krystle Campbell.

"I could hear Noah, I don't know how, but I could hear my little boy," she said. "He was saying, "Mommy, Mommy, Mommy,' over and over again. I said a prayer. I said, 'God, if this is it, take me, but let me know that Noah is OK.'"

Someone picked up her son and put him beside her.

Hours after her testimony, Gregory posted a defiant letter to Tsarnaev on her Facebook page: "TODAY ... I looked at you right in the face ... and realized I wasn't afraid anymore. And today I realized that sitting across from you was somehow the crazy kind of step forward that I needed all along. And I think that's the ironic thing that happens when someone intends something for evil. Because somehow, some way, it always ends up good."

She signed the letter, "Someone you shouldn't have messed with."

Karen Rand McWatters, Krystle Campbell's best friend, described how they happily strolled around Boston before heading to the finish line to watch McWatters' boyfriend cross.

A prosecutor showed her a photo of the two women taken in the hours before the explosion, both with huge smiles, McWatters with her arm around Campbell. Moments later, the two women were thrown to the sidewalk by the first explosion.

McWatters described how she inched across the pavement on her back to get to Krystle. Then the prosecutor showed her another photo of the two women lying on the sidewalk, their faces almost touching, both severely injured, Krystle dying.

"She very slowly said that her legs hurt, and we held hands, and shortly after that, her hand went limp in mine and she never spoke again after that," she said, choking back tears.

McWatters' left leg was amputated two days later. Somehow, she ended up with Krystle's cell phone in her pocket, triggering a cruel mix-up that led Campbell's family to believe for a time that she was still alive.

Another trial witness, Sydney Corcoran, 17 at the time of the bombings, told the jury that one minute she and her parents were happily waiting to see her aunt cross the finish line. The next, she was enveloped by smoke and was bleeding out on the sidewalk.

Boston Marathon bombing survivor Marc Fucarile, center, and his wife Jennifer, left, leave federal court. Fucarile lost his right leg in one of the explosions, March 4, 2015. (AP Photo/Michael Dwyer)

"I was getting increasingly cold," she said, "and I knew I was dying" -- before she was taken away and treated.

But later, in the hospital, a nurse gave her a warning before wheeling her mother into the room: "Your mother doesn't have her legs anymore."

AP Legal Affairs Writer Denise Lavoie, who covered the trial, was struck by the intensity of the survivors' stories. "I knew these people had suffered terribly, but I didn't know how bad it was until I heard them describe in their own words what they went through," Lavoie said. "I was stunned by their composure on the witness stand. I don't know if I could have kept it together as well as they did."

As Bill Richard took the witness stand, a palpable hush fell over the courtroom. Everyone knew this would be heartbreaking.

Quietly composed, he described how his family's annual excursion to watch the marathon turned into an unthinkable nightmare.

He and his wife, Denise, took their three children for ice cream just before picking a spot near the finish line to watch the runners come in. He said he could still remember what flavors each of the kids had, but Assistant U.S. Attorney Nadine Pellegrini gently told him he could keep that memory for himself.

He described a series of random decisions they made that day, bringing some in the courtroom to tears with his dignity and understated description: "I guess we were just unlucky that day."

They found a spot right up front, near a metal barricade that separated the crowd from the runners, a good perch for the kids. Martin, who was 8, and his 6-year-old sister, Jane, climbed on the bottom bar of the barricade to get a better view. Their 11-year-old brother, Henry, stood near Denise. Bill stood behind Jane and Martin.

When the first bomb exploded down the street, everyone was momentarily stunned, not knowing whether it was a manhole explosion or something worse. Richard said he and his wife decided quickly that they'd better get the kids and leave. Just then, the second bomb went off.

Richard looked around and saw injured people everywhere. But where was Jane, who had been right in front of him? His son, Henry, came running over to him, hugged him and said, "Is this really happening?"

Then Henry pointed to Jane, who was right behind him. One of her legs had been blown off.

Richard looked at Martin, lying on the sidewalk, as his wife knelt on the ground over him. He knew then his son wouldn't make it.

"I saw a little boy who had his body severely damaged by an explosion, and I just knew from what I saw that there was no chance," he said.

He scooped Jane up in one arm and took Henry in the other, trying to shield their eyes from the carnage around them as he took them across the street to get help. "I knew in my head that I needed to act quickly or we might not only lose Martin, but we might lose Jane, too," he said.

Pellegrini showed Richard a photo of his family, along with other people, standing near the barricade. One by one, Richard circled his family members for the jury, using a touch-screen monitor. Then Pellegrini circled another figure -- a young man wearing a white baseball cap backward -- standing a few feet behind Jane and Martin.

It was Dzhokhar Tsarnaev, just before the explosions.

Judy Clarke, Tsarnaev's lead defense lawyer, carefully laid the groundwork for the second phase of the trial, when -- after almost certain conviction -- the jury would be asked to decide Tsarnaev's punishment: life in prison or death by lethal injection.

She told the jury Tsarnaev was a 19-year-old kid at a difficult stage of his life and easily influenced by an older brother he admired. His parents had divorced and moved back to Russia. He was flunking out of college and had no family left in Cambridge except Tamerlan, who was living in the family's apartment with his wife and young daughter. He fell under the influence of his brother, who had become radicalized and sent him jihadist publications, recordings and lectures from his computer, she said.

Prosecutors countered that Dzhokhar was a willing participant who could have backed out of the plan at any time. Instead, they said, he stood in front of the Forum restaurant with one of the bombs in a backpack for a full four minutes and left it just feet from the Richard family and other children.

Tsarnaev appeared impassive during the trial. He stared straight ahead or looked down at the defense table most of the time, only occasionally glancing at the witnesses as they testified.

The jury of seven women and five men deliberated 11 hours over two days before returning the verdict: guilty on all 30 charges.

It was an anticlimactic moment. Now the only question was: Would they spare his life?

Support for that came from a surprising corner: little Martin's parents. In an emotional first-person plea published on the front page of The Boston Globe two years after the bombings, Bill and Denise Richard asked the Justice Department to take the death penalty off the table. It would spare them, they said, from having to relive their nightmare over and over through the long and tortuous legal review that inevitably follows any death decree.

"We understand all too well the heinousness and brutality of the crimes committed. We were there. We lived it. The defendant murdered our 8-year-old son, maimed our 7-year-old daughter, and stole part of our soul," they wrote.

But, they added, "We hope our two remaining children do not have to grow up with the lingering, painful reminder of what the defendant took from them, which years of appeals would undoubtedly bring."

The heavyset, gray-haired woman looked like a Russian babushka as she walked slowly to the witness stand. She seemed much older than her 64 years. Or maybe the pain etched on her face made her look decades older.

She looked at Tsarnaev, a nephew she adored but hadn't seen since he left Russia when he was 8. He wasn't a little boy anymore. Now, he was a convicted terrorist on trial for his life.

Patimat Suleimanova began weeping before Tsarnaev's lawyer could even ask the first question. She let out a huge sigh as she stared at him, then held her hand to her heart and began sobbing uncontrollably.

Then, for the first time since his trial began four months earlier, Tsarnaev showed some emotion. Grabbing a tissue, he dabbed quickly at his eyes and cheeks, wiping away tears as he looked at his heartbroken aunt. Later, after three of his cousins and another aunt testified, he blew a kiss to his family as he was led out of the courtroom by U.S. marshals.

Until then, Tsarnaev had sat stone-faced, looking straight ahead, seemingly disinterested. Even when bombing survivors described seeing their legs blown off or watching someone die, he gave away nothing about what he was feeling.

Now was the time to show emotion. This was the penalty phase of the trial, when the same jurors who convicted him would decide whether he should spend the rest of his life in prison or be executed.

This part of the trial had always been the focus for Tsarnaev's lawyers. They called to the stand every teacher, friend, classmate or relative they could find to talk about what a good kid he was. Among the adjectives used to describe him: "Kind." "Sweet." "Hard-working."

They showed photos of Tsarnaev as a young boy: with friends having pizza after a soccer tournament; holding his teacher's infant daughter; sitting on a bench with big brother Tamerlan. It was difficult to reconcile the photos of this happy, clean-cut little boy with the 21-year-old man sitting in court picking at his scraggly goatee and unkempt mass of curly hair.

Catheryn Charner-Laird, his third-grade teacher, smiled as she recalled a young boy just learning English after moving to the U.S. in 2002. He cared so much about his schoolwork, she said, and "always wanted to do the right thing."

Nabisat Suleimanova, a cousin of Dzhokhar Tsarnaev, leaves federal court in Boston after testifying during the penalty phase in Tsarnaev's trial, May 4, 2015. (AP Photo/Steven Senne)

His Russian cousins described a boy so charming he managed to soften up a stern aunt who had little patience for her other nieces and nephews. Once, while watching "The Lion King" with this particular aunt, Dzhokhar, about 5 at the time, cried during the scene when Simba's father, Mufasa, dies. His aunt was struck by Dzhokhar's sensitivity.

"She would say, 'I can't even understand how such a small child ... could sympathize so much, could understand tragedy,'" said Tsarnaev's cousin, Raisat Suleimanova.

AP's Lavoie wondered if these images would influence the jurors: "I couldn't stop thinking about the photos of this wide-eyed little boy. I kept going back to them in my mind and wondering how -- in a few short years -- he could go from that sweet little boy to a person who would put a bomb behind a group of kids."

The jury also heard about dysfunction and mental illness in Tsarnaev's family. A psychiatrist who treated his father, Anzor, in Boston said he suffered from post-traumatic stress disorder. Anzor told the psychiatrist he had been tortured in a Russian camp during the Chechen wars of the 1990s.

Relatives also described how Tsarnaev's mother, Zubeidat, went from a non-religious, high-fashion woman to a religious zealot who appeared to embrace a radical form of Islam and encouraged her sons to do the same.

Prosecutors used the penalty phase to remind the jury of the pain and suffering caused by Tsarnaev and his apparent defiance after the attack.

A blown-up photograph of Tsarnaev giving the middle finger to a camera in his cell was unveiled during opening statements. Prosecutors put the image in-between photos of the three bombing victims and the MIT police officer killed by the brothers days after the bombings. The photo was taken from a video of Tsarnaev in his holding cell on the day of his arraignment, three months after the bombings. His lawyers dismissed the gesture as typically immature teenage behavior.

Prosecutors ended their push for death by showing the jury photographs of the 17 people who became amputees, depicting them wearing prosthetic limbs, in wheelchairs and on crutches.

In a final heartbreaking scene, prosecutors played a video showing Denise Richard crouched over little Martin and resting her head on his chest as he lay dying on the sidewalk.

Steve Woolfenden sounded as if he was testifying through gritted teeth as he described frantically trying to get his 3-year-old son, Leo, out of his stroller after the second explosion. Woolfenden's left leg had been sheared off. As he lay helpless on the pavement, he saw Denise and Martin Richard next to him.

"I heard 'please' and 'Martin' being uttered by Denise Richard," he said. "Just pleading with her son." Begging him to live.

Martin bled to death on the sidewalk.

Tsarnaev's lawyers had a dramatic final witness of their own: Sister Helen Prejean, a nun and death penalty opponent made famous in the 1995 movie "Dead Man Walking."

Prejean told the jury she'd met with Tsarnaev five times since March. They discussed her religion, Roman Catholicism, and his, Islam. She told him about her work as a nun. They also talked about the death penalty, one of only two possible punishments he faced.

Did there come a time, his lawyer asked her, when he expressed his feelings about what happened to the victims in this case?

"He said it emphatically. He said, 'No one deserves to suffer like they did,'" Prejean said.

And there it was. If any of the 12 jurors was looking for a sign of regret from Tsarnaev, it was a nun from Louisiana who gave it to them. Tsarnaev never took the stand in his own defense.

Now Boylston Street was alive again. It was May 15, 2015: judgment day for Dzhokhar Tsarnaev, but commencement day for many in this city full of colleges.

Giddy graduates -- the young women in gaily colored dresses, the young men in suits -- chatted excitedly as they made their way along the busy street, some tossing their congratulatory bouquets on the marathon finish line as they passed by.

Just a few hours earlier, a jury had sentenced Tsarnaev to death by lethal injection.

The decision, though subject to years, perhaps decades of appeals, set the stage for what could be the nation's first execution of a terrorist in the post-9/11 era.

It came exactly two years and one month after Tsarnaev's bombs bloodied the very street where carefree coeds now skipped, embraced and headed to parties to drink, to dance, to celebrate their accomplishments and ponder their futures.

And now scrappy Boston could look ahead, too, sensing a measure of closure.

"Now he will go away and we will be able to move on. Justice. In his own words, 'an eye for an eye,'" said Sydney Corcoran, the young survivor who nearly bled to death and whose mother lost both legs.

Karen Brassard, injured by shrapnel along with her husband and daughter, offered words that spoke for an entire city:

"Today feels different only because it feels more complete. Right now, it feels like we can take a breath. We can breathe again."

--- This essay was written by Denise Lavoie and William J. Kole and edited by Christopher Sullivan.

Lavoie has been a Boston-based legal affairs writer for The Associated Press since 2003. She covered the marathon bombing drama from the first hours of the investigation through the manhunt and capture of Dzhokhar Tsarnaev – then covered his entire four-month trial in federal court. Kole, a former foreign correspondent for the AP and a veteran of 17 marathons, is AP's New England news editor, based in Boston. Sullivan is editor of AP's national reporting team.

1

PATRIOTS' DAY

The elite men start the 117th running of the Boston Marathon, in Hopkinton, Mass., April 15, 2013. (AP Photo/Stew Milne)

GOOD WEATHER AFTER 2012 HEAT
AT BOSTON MARATHON
April 14, 2013
By Jimmy Golen

The heat was unprecedented and so was the offer: Any of the 27,000 runners in last year's Boston Marathon could skip the race and automatically qualify for the 2013 edition instead.

About 2,300 people took race organizers up on the deal.

Smart move.

By re-starting their training and postponing their plans for a year, they are expected to be greeted with temperatures in the mid-50s on Monday (April 15) when the 117th Boston Marathon reaches Copley Square.

Perfect running weather was good news not just for the runners but for organizers coming off a year in which the record-setting heat sent record numbers of runners for medical attention.

"We got a bye," race director Dave McGillivray said this week. "And that's good, because we need this year to regroup."

A year after perfect weather helped pace Geoffrey Mutai to the fastest marathon in history, forecasts for the 2012 race climbed toward 90 degrees and Boston Athletic Association encouraged any inexperienced or ill runners to stay home. For those that decided to brave sweltering pavement that reached triple digits, extra water and doctors were available.

Winner Wesley Korir cramped up in the final mile but moved back into first place when those ahead of him faded even faster. His heat-slowed time of 2 hours, 12 minutes, 40 seconds was almost 10 minutes slower than Mutai's 2:03:02.

Sharon Cherop completed the Kenyan sweep, outkicking Jemima Jelagat Sumgong to win by 2 seconds in 2:31:50. The women's winner was decided by a sprint down Boylston Street for the fifth consecutive year all of them decided by 3 seconds or less.

Shalane Flanagan approaches the finish line to finish fourth in the women's division of the 2013 Boston Marathon, April 15, 2013. (AP Photo/Elise Amendola)

Both defending champions are back, leading a field that includes not just one American contender but two both on the women's side: Olympic bronze medalist Shalane Flanagan, of nearby Marblehead, and her training partner, Kara Goucher, a two-time Top 5 finisher here.

"I was a little girl, just north of here, and dreamed of running this race. It's surreal," said Flanagan, who finished second in the New York City Marathon in 2010 and finished 10th at the London Olympics. "I expect a hard run. I expect to die a thousand deaths. I don't know what to expect."

No U.S. runner has won the race since Lisa Larsen-Weidenbach took the women's title in 1985; the last American man to win was Greg Meyer in 1983. Jason Hartmann, who was fourth last year, is the top American contender on the men's side after Olympians Meb Keflezighi and Ryan Hall withdrew because of injuries.

"This needs to happen," Goucher said. "We want an American to win, period."

Korir, a Louisville alum, can continue a remarkable year for the Cardinals. After he won last year, Louisville followed that up with a victory in the Sugar Bowl and the men's basketball national championship while losing in the finals of the women's NCAA tournament.

Korir, who graduated in 2008, said he worked on the maintenance crew in the basketball team's dorm and knew Peyton Siva. He said watched the men's championship game against Michigan and drew inspiration from the Cardinals' late comeback.

"The way they are patient, the way they wait to kill the competition until the end of race, it's very educational," Korir said. "The winner is not the one that starts fastest. (That is) definitely my strategy."

Not long after the last of the sweaty and the sickened crossed the Back Bay finish line last year, B.A.A. officials gathered as always to discuss what they'd learned and how they can improve the next race. McGillivray said the keys were streamlining the ways they could ramp up the services in case of extreme heat: More water, more doctors, more buses to remove the ill or injured from the course.

That might come in handy someday.

Not this year.

"It's good that we don't have to implement it," McGillivray said after reciting the latest "wet bulb globe" forecast, which takes into account not just the temperature but also the humidity that can make it feel even hotter.

But not all the potential problems are weather-related. Last Monday, a week before the race, there was a water main break on the course near the start in Hopkinton and another near the finish in Boston.

Runners start the 117th running of the Boston Marathon, in Hopkinton, Mass., April 15, 2013. (AP Photo/Stew Milne)

"We spent 12 months planning for a 100-degree day because it could happen," McGillivray said. "You're planning for a weather event, and then something like this happens."

BOSTON MARATHON BOMBING KILLS AT LEAST 3, INJURES OVER 150
April 15, 2013
By Jimmy Golen

Two bombs exploded in the crowded streets near the finish line of the Boston Marathon on Monday (April 15), killing at least three people and injuring more than 140 in a bloody scene of shattered glass and severed limbs that raised alarms that terrorists might have struck again in the U.S.

A White House official speaking on condition of anonymity because the investigation was still unfolding said the attack was being treated as an act of terrorism.

President Barack Obama vowed that those responsible will "feel the full weight of justice."

As many as two unexploded bombs were also found near the end of the 26.2-mile course as part of what appeared to be a well-coordinated attack, but they were safely disarmed, according to a senior U.S. intelligence official, who also spoke on condition of anonymity because of the continuing investigation.

The fiery twin blasts took place about 10 seconds and about 100 yards apart, knocking spectators and at least one runner off their feet, shattering windows and sending dense plumes of smoke rising over the street and through the fluttering national flags lining the route. Blood stained the pavement, and huge shards were missing from window panes as high as three stories.

Medical workers aid the injured at the finish line of the 2013 Boston Marathon following explosions, April 15, 2013. (AP Photo/Charles Krupa)

"They just started bringing people in with no limbs," said runner Tim Davey of Richmond, Va. He said he and his wife, Lisa, tried to shield their children's eyes from the gruesome scene inside a medical tent that had been set up to care for fatigued runners, but "they saw a lot."

"They just kept filling up with more and more casualties," Lisa Davey said. "Most everybody was conscious. They were very dazed."

As the FBI took charge of the investigation, authorities shed no light on a motive or who may have carried out the bombings, and police said they had no suspects in custody. Officials in Washington said there was no immediate claim of responsibility.

Police said three people were killed. An 8-year-old boy was among the dead, according to a person who talked to a friend of the family and spoke on condition of anonymity.

Hospitals reported at least 144 people injured, at least 17 of them critically. The victims' injuries included broken bones, shrapnel wounds and ruptured eardrums.

At Massachusetts General Hospital, Alisdair Conn, chief of emergency services, said: "This is something I've never seen in my 25 years here ... this amount of carnage in the civilian population. This is what we expect from war."

Boston police clear an area near the finish line following the explosions, April 15, 2013. (AP Photo/Charles Krupa)

Some 23,000 runners took part in the race, one of the world's oldest and most prestigious marathons.

One of Boston's biggest annual events, the race winds up near Copley Square, not far from the landmark Prudential Center and the Boston Public Library. It is held on Patriots Day, which commemorates the first battles of the American Revolution, at Concord and Lexington in 1775.

Boston Police Commissioner Edward Davis asked people to stay indoors or go back to their hotel rooms and avoid crowds as bomb squads methodically checked parcels and bags left along the race route. He said investigators didn't know whether the bombs were hidden in mailboxes or trash cans.

He said authorities had received "no specific intelligence that anything was going to happen" at the race.

The Federal Aviation Administration barred low-flying aircraft within 3.5 miles of the site.

"We still don't know who did this or why," Obama said at the White House, adding, "Make no mistake: We will get to the bottom of this."

Medical workers wheel the injured across the finish line during the 2013 Boston Marathon, April 15, 2013. (AP Photo/Charles Krupa)

With scant official information to guide them, members of Congress said there was little or no doubt it was an act of terrorism.

"We just don't know whether it's foreign or domestic," said Rep. Michael McCaul, R-Texas, chairman of the House Committee on Homeland Security.

A few miles away from the finish line and around the same time, a fire broke out at the John F. Kennedy Library. The police commissioner said that it may have been caused by an incendiary device but that it was not clear whether it was related to the bombings.

The first explosion occurred on the north side of Boylston Street, just before the finish line, and some people initially thought it was a celebratory cannon blast.

When the second bomb went off, spectators' cheers turned to screams. As sirens blared, emergency workers and National Guardsmen who had been assigned to the race for crowd control began climbing over and tearing down temporary fences to get to the blast site.

The bombings occurred about four hours into the race and two hours after the men's winner crossed the finish line. By that point, more than 17,000 of the athletes had finished the marathon, but thousands more were still running.

An emergency responder and volunteers, including Carlos Arredondo, in the cowboy hat, push Jeff Bauman in a wheelchair after he was injured in one of two explosions, April 15, 2013. (AP Photo/Charles Krupa)

The attack may have been timed for maximum carnage: The four-hour mark is typically a crowded time near the finish line because of the slow-but-steady recreational runners completing the race and because of all the friends and relatives clustered around to cheer them on.

Runners in the medical tent for treatment of dehydration or other race-related ills were pushed out to make room for victims of the bombing.

A woman who was a few feet from the second bomb, Brighid Wall, 35, of Duxbury, said that when it exploded, runners and spectators froze, unsure of what to do. Her husband threw their children to the ground, lay on top of them and another man lay on top of them and said, "Don't get up, don't get up."

After a minute or so without another explosion, Wall said, she and her family headed to a Starbucks and out the back door through an alley. Around them, the windows of the bars and restaurants were blown out.

She said she saw six to eight people bleeding profusely, including one man who was kneeling, dazed, with blood trickling down his head. Another person was on the ground covered in blood and not moving.

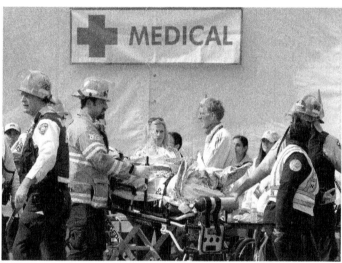

Medical personnel work outside the medical tent in the aftermath of two blasts which exploded near the finish line of the Boston Marathon in Boston, Monday, April 15, 2013. (AP Photo/Elise Amendola)

"My ears are zinging. Their ears are zinging," Wall said. "It was so forceful. It knocked us to the ground."

Competitors and race volunteers were crying as they fled the chaos. Authorities went onto the course to carry away the injured, while race stragglers were rerouted away from the smoking site.

Roupen Bastajian, a state trooper from Smithfield, R.I., had just finished the race when he heard the blasts.

"I started running toward the blast. And there were people all over the floor," he said. "We started grabbing tourniquets and started tying legs. A lot of people amputated. ... At least 25 to 30 people have at least one leg missing, or an ankle missing, or two legs missing."

The race honored the victims of the Newtown, Conn., shooting with a special mile marker in Monday's race.

Boston Athletic Association president Joanne Flaminio previously said there was "special significance" to the fact that the race is 26.2 miles long and 26 people died at Sandy Hook Elementary School.

OBAMA: 'WE WILL FIND OUT WHO DID THIS'
April 15, 2013
By Julie Pace

President Barack Obama urged a nervous nation to avoid jumping to conclusions about Monday's explosions at the Boston Marathon, while acknowledging that officials "still do not know who did this or why." A White House official later said the incident was being treated as terrorism.

Speaking from the White House just three hours after the explosions, Obama was cautious in his remarks, stopping short of calling the incident an act of terror.

Obama said the explosions were the act of an individual or group, but vowed to hold those responsible accountable.

President Barack Obama speaks in the James Brady Press Briefing Room at the White House in Washington following the explosions at the marathon in Boston, April 15, 2013. (AP Photo/Charles Dharapak)

"We will find out who did this. We'll find out why they did this," Obama said in his brief, three-minute statement. "Any responsible individuals, any responsible groups, will feel the full weight of justice."

The White House official spoke on condition of anonymity because the investigation was ongoing.

The president said the government would increase security around the United States "as necessary" but did not say whether his administration thought the incident was part of a larger plot.

Massachusetts Gov Deval Patrick, right, listens as Boston Mayor Tom Menino, left, speaks about the explosions during a press conference, April 15, 2013. (AP Photo/Bizuayehu Tesfaye)

Obama did not offer specific details on deaths or injuries, saying only that multiple people had been wounded, some of them gravely.

Authorities say at least two people were killed and more than 80 injured during two explosions near the finish of the marathon. A senior U.S. intelligence official said two other explosive devices were found near the end of the 26.2-mile course.

BOSTON'S BELOVED DAY, DISSOLVED IN CHAOS AND TEARS
April 16, 2013
By Meghan Barr and Adam Geller

It dawned chilly, clear and blue, a parsimonious but perfect serving of New England springtime that because it came on the third Monday in April unquestionably called for a celebration.

The kind of morning just right for an 11:05 a.m. first pitch at Fenway Park. A day to remind your kids about the heroes of the American Revolution before heading out to stake a place on the curb and cheer on modern-day heroes of the Marathon. A day, Bostonians say, when their city realizes the best of itself.

And then, in 10 seconds of fury and smoke, the joy founded upon 117 years of sweat and aspiration was stolen away.

Blood covers the sidewalk on Boylston Street, at the site where a bomb exploded during the 2013 Boston Marathon in front of the Marathon Sports store in Boston, April 15, 2013. (AP Photo/Charles Krupa)

When a pair of bombs exploded Monday (April 15) near the finish line of the Boston Marathon, killing at least three people and injuring more than 140, it left a scene of shattered glass and severed limbs that terrorized this city. Spectators who moments before had been cheering family and friends were knocked to the ground. Blood stained the pavement. With reports that two more bombs had been found unexploded, Bostonians and visitors hunkered down in fear.

But to appreciate the totality of what Boston surrendered in those moments of horror requires understanding just how much the city had to lose. Other cities have, no doubt, experienced far more horrific tragedies. But few have had their sense of security ripped away at a moment of such singular exultation, on a day that captures an essential part of this city's soul.

Medical workers aid the injured at the finish line of the 2013 Boston Marathon following two explosions that shattered the euphoria of the day, April 15, 2013. (AP Photo/Charles Krupa)

Monday (April 15) in Boston was Patriots' Day, a holiday unique to New England that brings the region's rich history alive with reenactments recalling the battles of Lexington and Concord that marked the beginning of the American Revolution. For the city's children, it means a day off from school as they begin Spring Break. For 23,000 runners from around the world, the day caps months spent preparing to test body and spirit. It is a day when a city feels like a village, when strangers offer high-fives and free food to runners they'll never see again.

When it's over, runners wander through the streets, proudly wearing medals bearing the image of a unicorn. It is a symbol chosen because it represents the endless pursuit of perfection that lives mostly in myth except, that is, in those all-too-brief hours when Boston finds a bit of perfection in itself.

To see all that shattered is a hard feeling to put in to words, Bostonians say. But they tried nonetheless, because it felt right to do so.

For Meredith Saillant, the day's transformation was summed up in minutes, just after she finished running the 26.2-mile race, when a gathering with friends in a hotel room overlooking the finish line morphed from a party-in-the-making into a search for an escape route.

"I went into the shower laughing, so happy about what this day was all about and I came out and it was all over," said Saillant, who lives in the Boston suburb of Brookline. "It's just that sense of completely feeling just vulnerable, like something's been taken from us for no reason, for absolutely no reason, and it's just completely senseless."

In an old city that prides itself on its institutions, workers at Boston's hospitals seemed stunned by the shrapnel wounds and ruptured eardrums, as much because of the timing and the place they were inflicted as for their severity.

"This is something I've never seen in my 25 years here," said Alisdair Conn, chief of emergency services at Massachusetts General Hospital. "This amount of carnage in the civilian population, this is what we expect from war."

But the pain and despair was hardly limited to the emergency wards. Instead, it spread across the city, echoing off empty cobblestones.

By evening, SWAT team members with machine guns patrolled hospitals and stood outside hotels that were on lockdown. Most bars had closed early on a night when they're typically packed with post-race revelers.

"Be Safe and be (hash) Boston Strong," read one sign posted on the door of a darkened bar. "We urge everyone to please stay safe," said the sign posted at another.

At The Hill Tavern, across the street from Massachusetts General, people hunched over their beers and stared in shock at the television screens broadcasting news of the explosions. The mood was somber.

An unidentified Boston Marathon runner is comforted as she cries in the aftermath of two blasts which exploded near the finish line of the Boston Marathon, April 15, 2013. (AP Photo/Elise Amendola)

"You don't ever think something like this would happen so close to home, especially in Boston," said 23-year-old Kaitlyn Kloeblen. "You always think it's such a small, safe city."

Kloeblen said she was avoiding the subway system and staying close to home for the night. "We don't want to go anywhere on the T or anything," she said. "We don't really feel safe."

The mood was equally wan in the promenades around historic Faneuil Hall and Quincy Market that would normally be thronged with post-Marathon partiers. Instead, nearly all the bars and restaurants were black, surrendering the streetscape to a few lonely hangers-on, a handful of police officers and a bronze statue of Red Auerbach, the legendary Celtics coach and general manager.

"Today is a very special day. I'm from Boston and I'm devastated," said Laura Gassett, who had brought friends from California, Utah and England to the Marathon before seeking solace at Durgin Park, one of just two bars open. "The terrorists are getting exactly what they wanted. They want to shut Boston down and they did. They cut us off right at the knees."

An unidentified Boston Marathon runner leaves the course crying near Copley Square in Boston, April 15, 2013. (AP Photo/Winslow Townson)

As Gassett and her friends went in search of a cab, a chain across the entrance to Dick's Last Resort a bar that posts its closing time as "til I freakin' say so!!" swung in the breeze and an outdoor loudspeaker broadcast the notes of "Always and Forever," across the emptiness that was not supposed to be.

"We were sitting in the bar and we saw bomb squads walking by with M-16s, checking trash barrels," said Gassett's partner, Candy Shoemaker. "It was like, `Oh my God.'"

The disbelief seemed most obvious in the faces and the voices of runners. Many recalled how the day had started off so perfectly with cool, clear skies after last year's stifling heat.

"The runners on the course were happy," said Lucretia Ausse, who was running her first Boston Marathon, "and it was wild going through Wellesley. Just everybody - the spectators were off the hook."

Ausse had just crossed the finish line when she turned around and saw smoke pouring into the sky.

Justine Franco of Montpelier, Vt., holds up a sign near Copley Square in Boston looking for her missing friend, April, who was running in her first Boston Marathon. Two bombs exploded near the finish line of the marathon on Monday, killing at least two people and injuring at least 23 others, April 15, 2013. (AP Photo/Winslow Townson)

The finish line is usually a joyous place in Boston: the ultimate accomplishment in a marathon that's considered among the most difficult in the world to run, owing to its steep hills and competitive qualifying times. But this time, runners surged away from the finish line, anxious to pick up phones that would allow them to reassure their families. Except that none of the calls were going through.

There was anxiety and fear in Boston Common, a historic park just beyond the finish line where runners wrapped in foil blankets usually eagerly reunite with family members.

Instead, people wandered in and out in a confused daze, searching for family and friends who were unreachable. Sirens rang through the air. Helicopters thundered overhead. Runners collapsed on the ground, crying.

"It was mayhem. It was chaotic," said Mike Ferrari, 24, who lives in Boston. "Everyone just started running."

By nightfall, nearly all had departed and runner Tara Redmond, 42, hurried back to her hotel through eerily quiet streets. Tonight, after months of training to earn a Marathon medal, it felt wrong to wear hers as if there was something to celebrate. The only reason she had it on at all was that her mother had told her she deserved it. But Redmond was no longer sure.

Women react as they walk from the area where there was an explosion after the Boston Marathon in Boston, April 15, 2013. (AP Photo/Josh Reynolds)

She talked about all her fellow runners who'd joined Boston's once-a-year chase of excellence and who had been unable to claim their rightful prize. Together, with this city, they had started the day that held such promise, only to see it evaporate.

"It's such a sad day," Redmond said. Then, she glanced down, running her fingers over the medal the one depicting the Unicorn that symbolizes a city's search for rarely attainable perfection and her eyes filled with tears.

2

INVESTIGATION AND MANHUNT

An investigator in a protective suit examines debris on Boylston Street in Boston, as investigation of the Boston Marathon bombings continues, April 18, 2013. (AP Photo/Elise Amendola)

FBI SEEKS IMAGES IN BOSTON MARATHON BOMB INQUIRY
April 16, 2013
By Jimmy Golen

Investigators appealed to the public Tuesday (April 16) for amateur video and photos that might yield clues to the Boston Marathon bombing as the chief FBI agent in Boston vowed "we will go to the ends of the Earth" to find whoever carried out the deadly attack.

Two bombs blew up seconds apart Monday (April 15) at the finish line of one of the world's most storied races, tearing off limbs and leaving the streets spattered with blood and strewn with broken glass. Three people were killed, including an 8-year-old boy, and more than 170 were wounded.

A doctor treating the wounded said one of the victims was maimed by what looked like ball bearings or BBs.

Federal investigators said no one had claimed responsibility for the bombings, which took place on one of the city's biggest civic holidays, Patriots Day. But the blasts raised the specter of another terrorist attack on U.S. soil.

President Barack Obama said the bombings were an act of terrorism, but investigators do not know if they were carried out by an international organization, domestic group or a "malevolent individual." He added: "The American people refuse to be terrorized."

Across the U.S., from Washington to Los Angeles, police tightened security, monitoring landmarks, government buildings, transit hubs and sporting events. Security was especially tight in Boston, with bomb-sniffing dogs checking Amtrak passengers' luggage at South Station and transit police patrolling with rifles.

Blast site for first bomb on Boylston Street near the finish line, April 15, 2013. (AP Photo/Elise Amendola)

"They can give me a cavity search right now and I'd be perfectly happy," said Daniel Wood, a video producer from New York City who was waiting for a train.

Richard DesLauriers, FBI agent in charge in Boston, said investigators had received "voluminous tips" and were interviewing witnesses and analyzing the crime scene.

"We will go to the ends of the Earth to identify the subject or subjects who are responsible for this despicable crime, and we will do everything we can to bring them to justice," he said.

Gov. Deval Patrick said that contrary to earlier reports, no unexploded bombs were found. He said the only explosives were the ones that went off.

Blast site for second bomb on Boylston Street one day after bombing, April 16, 2013. (AP Photo/Elise Amendola)

FBI agents searched an apartment in the Boston suburb of Revere overnight, and investigators were seen leaving with brown paper bags, plastic trash bags and a duffel bag. But it was unclear whether the tenant had anything to do with the attack.

A law enforcement official who spoke on condition of anonymity because he was not authorized to release details of the investigation said the man had been tackled by a bystander, then police, as he ran from the scene of the explosions.

But he said it is possible the man was simply running away to protect himself from the blast, as many others did.

At a news conference, police and federal agents repeatedly appealed for any video, audio and photos taken by marathon spectators, even images that people might not think are significant.

"There has to be hundreds, if not thousands, of photos and videos" that might help investigators, state police Col. Timothy Alben said.

Boston Police Commissioner Edward Davis said investigators also gathered a large number of surveillance tapes from businesses in the area and intend to go through the video frame by frame.

"This is probably one of the most photographed areas in the country yesterday," he said.

Investigators refused to give any specifics on the bombs and say, for example, where they might have been hidden or whether they were packed with shrapnel for maximum carnage, as is often the case in terror bombings overseas.

David Green holds his iPad showing the photo he took shortly after the Boston Marathon bombings, at his home in Jacksonville, Fla. Seconds after the Boston Marathon bombs exploded, Green pulled out his smartphone and took a photo of the chaos developing a couple hundred yards in front of him -- the smoke, the people running in panic. That photo put Green, the CEO of 110% Play Harder, a sportswear company, in the national media spotlight, April 19, 2013. (AP Photo/Phil Sears)

But Dr. Stephen Epstein of the emergency medicine department at Beth Israel Deaconess Medical Center said he saw an X-ray of one victim's leg that had "what appears to be small, uniform, round objects throughout it similar in the appearance to BBs."

The fiery explosions took place about 10 seconds and about 100 yards apart, knocking spectators and at least one runner off their feet, shattering windows and sending columns of smoke rising over the street.

Roupen Bastajian, a state trooper from Smithfield, R.I., had just finished the race when he heard the explosions.

"I started running toward the blast. And there were people all over the floor," he said. "We started grabbing tourniquets and started tying legs. A lot of people amputated."

At least 17 people were critically injured, police said. At least eight children were being treated at hospitals. In addition to losing limbs, victims suffered broken bones, shrapnel wounds and ruptured eardrums.

At Massachusetts General Hospital, Alasdair Conn, chief of emergency services, said: "This is something I've never seen in my 25 years here ... this amount of carnage in the civilian population. This is what we expect from war."

Eight-year-old Martin Richard was among the dead, said U.S. Rep. Stephen Lynch, a family friend. The boy's mother, Denise, and 6-year-old sister, Jane, were badly injured. His brother and father were also watching the race but were not hurt.

A candle burned on the stoop of the family's single-family home in the city's Dorchester section Tuesday, and the word "Peace" was written in chalk on the front walk.

Neighbor Betty Delorey said Martin loved to climb the neighborhood trees, and hop the fence outside his home.

Tim Davey of Richmond, Va., was with his wife, Lisa, and children near a medical tent that had been set up to care for fatigued runners when the injured began arriving. "They just started bringing people in with no limbs," he said.

"Most everybody was conscious," Lisa Davey said. "They were very dazed."

The Boston Marathon is one of the world's oldest and most prestigious races and about 23,000 runners participated. Most of them had crossed the finish line by the time the bombs exploded, but thousands more were still completing the course.

The attack may have been timed for maximum bloodshed: The four-hour mark is typically a crowded time near the finish line because of the slow-but-steady recreational runners completing the race and because of all the friends and relatives clustered around to cheer them on.

Davis, the police commissioner, said authorities had received "no specific intelligence that anything was going to happen" at the race. On Tuesday, he said that two security sweeps of the route had been conducted before the marathon.

The race winds up near Copley Square, not far from the landmark Prudential Center and the Boston Public Library. It is held on Patriots Day, which commemorates the first battles of the American Revolution, at Concord and Lexington in 1775.

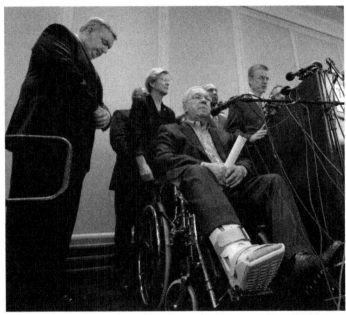

Boston Mayor Thomas Menino, below, sits in a wheelchair as he and Boston Police Commissioner Ed Davis, far left, listen to FBI Special Agent in Charge Richard DesLauriers, far right, speak during a news conference in Boston, April 16, 2013. (AP Photo/Elise Amendola)

Richard Barrett, the former U.N. coordinator for an al-Qaida and Taliban monitoring team who has also worked for British intelligence, said the relatively small size of the devices in Boston and the timing of the blasts suggest a domestic attack rather than an al-Qaida-inspired one.

"This happened on Patriots Day it is also the day Americans are supposed to have their taxes in and Boston is quite a symbolic city," said Barrett, now senior director at the Qatar International Academy for Security Studies.

The Pakistani Taliban, which has threatened attacks in the United States because of its support for the Pakistani government, on Tuesday denied any role in the bombings.

A woman who was a few feet from the second bomb, Brighid Wall, 35, of Duxbury, said that when it exploded, runners and spectators froze, unsure of what to do. Her husband threw their children to the ground, lay on top of them and another man lay on top of them and said, "Don't get up, don't get up."

After a minute or so without another explosion, Wall said, she and her family headed to a Starbucks and out the back door through an alley. Around them, the windows of the bars and restaurants were blown out.

She said she saw six to eight people bleeding profusely, including one man who was kneeling, dazed, with blood trickling down his head. Another person was on the ground covered in blood and not moving.

"My ears are zinging. Their ears are zinging," Wall said. "It was so forceful. It knocked us to the ground."

VIDEO FOOTAGE SHOWS BOMB SUSPECT
April 18, 2013
By Denise Lavoie and Rodrique Ngowi

In what could be major break in the Boston Marathon case, investigators are on the hunt for a man seen in a department store surveillance video dropping off a bag at the site of the bombings, a local politician said Wednesday (April 17).

Separately, a law enforcement official confirmed that authorities have found an image of a potential suspect but don't know his name.

The development less than 48 hours after the attack, which left three people dead and more than 170 wounded marked a possible turning point in a case that has investigators analyzing photos and videos frame by frame for clues to who carried out the twin bombings and why.

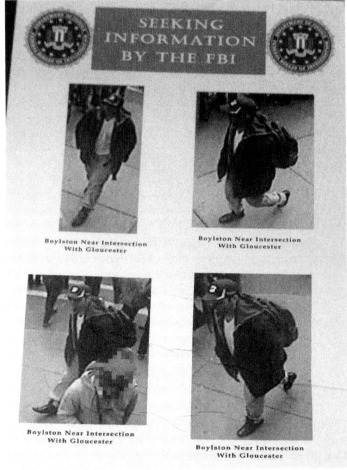

Photos of one of two suspects sought in the Boston Marathon bombing is displayed during a news conference talking about the investigation of the Boston Marathon explosions, April 18, 2013. (AP Photo/Julio Cortez)

City Council President Stephen Murphy, who said he was briefed by Boston police, said investigators saw the image on surveillance footage they got from a department store near the finish line and matched the findings with witness descriptions of someone leaving the scene.

"I know it's very active and very fluid right now that they are on the chase," Murphy said. He added: "They may be on the verge of arresting someone, and that's good."

The bombs were crudely fashioned from ordinary kitchen pressure cookers packed with explosives, nails and ball bearings, investigators and others close to the case said. Investigators suspect the devices were then hidden in black duffel bags and left on the ground.

As a result, they were looking for images of someone lugging a dark, heavy bag.

One department store video "has confirmed that a suspect is seen dropping a bag near the point of the second explosion and heading off," Murphy said.

A law enforcement official who was not authorized to discuss the case publicly and spoke to The Associated Press on the condition of anonymity confirmed only that investigators had an image of a potential suspect whose name was not known to them and who had not been questioned.

Several media outlets reported that a suspect had been identified from surveillance video taken at a Lord & Taylor department store between the sites of the bomb blasts.

The turn of events came with Boston in a state of high excitement over conflicting reports of a breakthrough.

A law enforcement official briefed on the investigation told the AP around midday that a suspect was in custody. The official, who was not authorized to divulge details of the investigation and spoke on the condition of anonymity, said the suspect was expected in federal court. But the FBI and the U.S. attorney's office in Boston said no arrests had been made.

By nightfall, there was no evidence anyone was in custody. No one was taken to court. The law enforcement official, who had affirmed there was a suspect in custody even after federal officials denied it, was unable to obtain any further information or explanation.

At least 14 bombing victims, including three children, remained in critical condition. Dozens of victims have been released from hospitals, and officials at three hospitals that treated some of the most seriously injured said they expected all their remaining patients to survive. A 2-year-old boy with a head injury was improving and might go home Thursday, Boston Children's Hospital said.

On Wednesday, investigators in white jumpsuits fanned out across the streets, rooftops and awnings around the blast site in search of clues. They picked through trash cans, plastic cup sleeves and discarded sports drink dispensers.

Investigators comb through the scene of the second blast site, April 17, 2013. (AP Photo/Julio Cortez)

Boston remained under a heavy security presence, and some people admitted they were nervous about moving about in public spaces.

Tyler King, a personal trainer from Attleboro who works in Boston, said four of five clients canceled on him a day earlier because they were worried about venturing into the city. He took the train in, but "I kind of kept my head on a swivel."

Kenya Nadry, a website designer, took her 5-year-old nephew to a playground.

"There's still some sense of fear, but I feel like Boston's resilient," she said. "The fine men in blue will take care of a lot of it."

Police were stationed on street corners across downtown Boston, while National Guardsmen set up tents on the Boston Common and stationed tactical vehicles.

Dr. Horacio Hojman, associate chief of trauma at Tufts Medical Center, said patients were in surprisingly good spirits when they were brought in.

"Despite what they witnessed, despite what they suffered, despite many of them having life-threatening injuries, their spirits were not broken," he said. "And I think that should probably be the message for all of us that this horrible act of terror will not bring us down."

President Barack Obama and his challenger in the last election, former Massachusetts Gov. Mitt Romney, planned to visit Boston on Thursday to attend a service honoring the victims.

The blasts killed 8-year-old Martin Richard, of Boston, and 29-year-old Krystle Campbell, of Medford. The Shenyang Evening News, a state-run Chinese newspaper, identified the third victim as Lu Lingzi, a graduate student at Boston University.

ITS STREETS DESERTED, AN UNEASY
BOSTON PERSEVERES
April 19, 2013
By Allen G. Breed

The Red Sox and the Bruins both scrapped their games. The famous Quincy Market at Faneuil Hall was closed, and there were more pigeons than tourists on City Hall Plaza. Even the Starbucks at Government Center was shuttered.

The killing of one suspected Boston Marathon bomber and the manhunt for another brought life in large swaths of the notoriously gridlocked Beantown to a screeching halt for most of the day, leaving residents and tourists alike frustrated and angry.

"It took me an hour and a half to find a coffee this morning," Daniel Miller, a financier from New York, said as he wandered the desolate plaza beside a statue of patriot Samuel Adams. "I was joking with a person that I guess the strategy is we'll make this person not be able to get a coffee in the morning, and maybe they'll give up."

For Steve Parlin, who is staying at a veteran's shelter on Court Street, in the shadow of City Hall, the scene was nothing to joke about.

"Helicopters are flying over," the Gulf War-era Coast Guard veteran said as he strolled across the plaza, a bottle of water in his hand. "Everything's closed. It's creepy. Machine guns. Creepy."

Gov. Deval Patrick, Mayor Thomas Menino and Boston Police Commissioner Edward Davis ordered all people in the city of Boston to shelter in place. Several area colleges and universities were locked down. Commuter rail, bus and subway service were suspended, and thousands of workers were told to stay home. The restrictions were lifted about an hour before sunset.

Even before that, the owners of the Lower Depths tap room in the heart of the Boston University area tweeted that they were opening for dinner.

"The owner felt like time had passed and still nothing. No news, no anything," general manager Jenna Figueiredo said. "So why should we just continue to stay hidden from somebody who's out to harm us? Why not just open up to the public and let people live their normal lives and not let a threat like this disturb our everyday lives, you know?"

The streets and sidewalks around Faneuil Hall Marketplace in Boston are almost deserted at dinnertime as a call for "shelter-in-place" for Boston and some area communities remains in force. Massachusetts Gov. Deval Patrick says the decision to lock down much of greater Boston during the search for the surviving suspect in the Boston Marathon bombings was a "tough call" but one he's glad that was made, April 19, 2013. (AP Photo/Elise Amendola)

For Kathy Hall and her daughter, Danielle, who spent 24 hours together in Danielle's one-room apartment, the reprieve couldn't have come soon enough.

"We're very happy," the mother said between bites of a fish wrap and sips of beer. "She only had mac and cheese, right? So that's all we had all day pretty much."

The potential impact on businesses and the local economy was not immediately clear. Jon Hurst, President of the Massachusetts Retailers Association, said he had no estimate yet.

"Certainly it is in the tens of millions for retail and restaurants, and in hundreds of millions in lost productivity when adding in offices, etc.," he wrote in an email to the AP.

Filming for director David O. Russell's movie "American Hustle" was halted because of the manhunt and lockdown. The mayhem also interrupted Dallas couple Tom and Vy Nguyen's fifth wedding anniversary trip to the city.

The couple was hoping to visit the Museum of Fine Art, Fenway Park and several other landmarks. Instead, they were having a hard time just finding a restaurant that was open.

"I just want to eat," Tom Nguyen, 32, a health-care company analyst, said as they passed the normally raucous Big Apple Circle big top at Government Center. "I've never seen a city shut down like this for one person. This is very bizarre for us."

A sign calling for citizens of Boston to "Shelter in Place" is shown on I-93 in Boston as the manhunt intensified for a young man described as a dangerous terrorist, April 19, 2013. (AP Photo/Elise Amendola)

One place that did not shut down was the Union Oyster House, which bills itself as "America's oldest restaurant." But it was definitely easier to find a table than during your typical lunchtime.

Several people hunched over seafood and beers around the semicircular bar, and only a few tables upstairs were occupied. Manager Troy Thissell said that didn't matter.

"The city of Boston said do the best you can do. Our choice. So we chose to open," said Thissell, who was sporting a "Boston Strong" button on his shirt. "We've always in the past. During blizzards and other things, we do open. And we're going to continue to do so.

For people accustomed to the bustle of this "big small town," the quiet was unsettling.

"We just went to get a cup of coffee, and there's no line at Dunkin' Donuts," said electrician Joe Gore, who was sipping his java on a picnic table near Rowes Wharf, where he was helping wire a new Starbucks. "So it's pretty scary quiet."

Many people seemed to understand the drastic measures. But others considered it ridiculous.

Miller recently moved to New York after spending the past five years in Israel. As the 29-year-old in the black yarmulke strolled through the city's Holocaust memorial, he couldn't help feeling that officials here were overreacting.

"You know, when Israel gets one rocket attack, let's say it injures three people," he said. "It's terrible. This event, thank God it only killed three people. And it injured a lot of people. If a rocket attack injures five people, 10 people in Israel and kills one person, we think, `Oh, thank God it only killed one person. It didn't kill 50 people.'"

Miller understands that this kind of event is still relatively rare in the United States, and unheard of in Boston. But he said this is the kind of mayhem terrorists want, and Boston is giving it to them.

"Hopefully, Americans will realize what Israelis have to go through and have more solidarity for them and understand when they fight back and retaliate," he said. "Because that's exactly what Boston's doing today. They're going and doing everything possible in order to get this one person. The city has come to a halt in order to get this one person."

Scott Lapworth drove in from Thompson, Ct., to do a wallpapering job near the waterfront Friday morning and noticed that the commute was not nearly as hairy as usual.

"I don't think I've ever seen it so deserted down here," he said as he chewed a ham and cheese sandwich on the steps beside Faneuil Hall.

"It's unfortunate that these type of people are around, but it's not going to keep me from coming to work or going to places to eat in public or stuff," he said, munching on chips. "I'm not going to let them change MY lifestyle."

Jesse Bonelli, a video game artist who lives in locked-down Watertown, stayed inside his house and sharpened a machete just in case.

"It's something I usually keep hanging on the wall, but it's the only weapon I have," said Bonelli, 23. "I want to be ready in case anyone bursts into the house. After everything that happened this week, I keep wondering what's next."

BOSTON MARATHON SUSPECT CORNERED
IN BACKYARD BOAT
April 20, 2013
By Jay Lindsay and Eileen Sullivan

A police officer evacuates woman holding a child as members of law enforcement conduct a search in Watertown, Mass., April 19, 2013. (AP Photo/Matt Rourke)

For just a few minutes, it seemed like the dragnet that had shut down a metropolitan area of millions while legions of police went house to house looking for the suspected Boston Marathon bomber had failed.

Weary officials lifted a daylong order that had kept residents in their homes, saying it was fruitless to keep an entire city locked down. Then one man emerged from his home and noticed blood on the pleasure boat parked in his backyard. He lifted the tarp and found the wounded 19-year-old college student known the world over as Suspect No. 2.

Soon after that, the 24-hour drama that paralyzed a city and transfixed a nation was over.

Dzhokhar Tsarnaev's capture touched off raucous celebrations in and around Boston, with chants of "USA, USA" as residents flooded the streets in relief and jubilation after four tense days since twin explosions ripped through the marathon's crowd at the finish line, killing three people and wounding more than 180.

A woman carries a girl from their home as a SWAT team searching for a suspect in the Boston Marathon bombings enters the building in Watertown, Mass., April 19, 2013. (AP Photo/Charles Krupa)

The 19-year-old whose older brother and alleged accomplice was killed earlier that morning in a wild shootout in suburban Boston was hospitalized in serious condition Saturday, unable to be questioned to determine his motives. U.S. officials said a special interrogation team for high-value suspects would question him without reading him his Miranda rights, invoking a rare public safety exception triggered by the need to protect police and the public from immediate danger.

President Barack Obama said there are many unanswered questions about the Boston bombings, including whether the two men had help from others. He urged people not to rush judgment about their motivations.

Dzhokhar and his brother, 26-year-old Tamerlan Tsarnaev, were identified by authorities and relatives as ethnic Chechens from southern Russia who had been in the U.S. for about a decade and were believed to be living in Cambridge, just outside Boston. Tamerlan Tsarnaev died in the shootout early in the day of gunshot wounds and a possible blast injury. At one point, he was run over by his younger brother in a car as he lay wounded, according to investigators.

During a long night of violence Thursday and into Friday, the brothers killed an MIT police officer, severely wounded another lawman during a gun battle and hurled explosives at police in a desperate getaway attempt, authorities said.

Late Friday, less than an hour after authorities lifted the lockdown, they tracked down the younger man holed up in the boat, weakened by a gunshot wound after fleeing on foot from the overnight shootout with police that left 200 spent rounds behind.

The resident who spotted Dzhokhar Tsarnaev in his boat in his Watertown yard called police, who tried to talk the suspect into getting out of the boat, said Boston Police Commissioner Ed Davis.

"He was not communicative," Davis said.

Instead, he said, there was an exchange of gunfire the final volley of one of the biggest manhunts in American history.

The violent endgame unfolded just a day after the FBI released surveillance-camera images of two young men suspected of planting the pressure-cooker explosives at the marathon's finish line, an attack that put the nation on edge for the week.

Watertown residents who had been told in the morning to stay inside behind locked doors poured out of their homes and lined the streets to cheer police vehicles as they rolled away from the scene.

Police officers aim their weapons in Watertown, April 19, 2013. (AP Photo/Matt Rourke)

Investigators work near the location in Watertown, Mass. where the previous night police captured Dzhokhar Tsarnaev, 19, the surviving Boston Marathon bombing suspect, in a backyard boat after a wild car chase and gun battle earlier in the day left his older brother dead, April 20, 2013. (AP Photo/Katie Zezima)

Celebratory bells rang from a church tower. Teenagers waved American flags. Drivers honked. Every time an emergency vehicle went by, people cheered loudly.

"They finally caught the jerk," said nurse Cindy Boyle. "It was scary. It was tense."

Police said three other people were taken into custody for questioning at an off-campus housing complex at the University of the Massachusetts at Dartmouth where the younger man may have lived.

"Tonight, our family applauds the entire law enforcement community for a job well done, and trust that our justice system will now do its job," said the family of 8-year-old Martin Richard, who died in the bombing.

The FBI was swamped with tips 300,000 per minute after the release of the surveillance-camera photos, but what role those played in the overnight clash was unclear. State Police spokesman Dave Procopio said police realized they were dealing with the bombing suspects based on what the two men told a carjacking victim during their night of crime.

A police officer gives a thumbs up to another officer in Watertown, Mass. after the second of two suspects in the Boston Marathon bombing was captured and taken into custody after a manhunt that left the city virtually paralyzed, April 19, 2013. (AP Photo/Craig Ruttle)

The search by thousands of law enforcement officers all but shut down the Boston area for much of the day. Officials halted all mass transit, including Amtrak trains to New York, advised businesses not to open, and warned close to 1 million people in the entire city and some of its suburbs to unlock their doors only for uniformed police.

Around midday, the suspects' uncle, Ruslan Tsarni of Montgomery Village, Md., pleaded on television: "Dzhokhar, if you are alive, turn yourself in and ask for forgiveness."

Until the younger man's capture, it was looking like a grim day for police. As night fell, they announced that they were scaling back the hunt and lifting the stay-indoors order across the region because they had come up empty-handed.

But then the break came and within a couple of hours, the search was over. Dzhokhar Tsarnaev was captured about a mile from the site of the shootout that killed his brother.

A neighbor described how heavily armed police stormed by her window not long after the lockdown was lifted the rapid report of gunshots left her huddled on the bathroom floor on top of her young son.

"I was just waiting for bullets to just start flying everywhere," Deanna Finn said.

When at last the gunfire died away and Dzhokhar Tsarnaev was taken from the neighborhood in an ambulance, an officer gave Finn a cheery thumbs-up.

"To see the look on his face, he was very, very happy, so that made me very, very happy," she said.

Authorities said the man dubbed Suspect No. 1 the one in sunglasses and a dark baseball cap in the surveillance-camera pictures - was Tamerlan Tsarnaev, while Suspect No. 2, the one in a white baseball cap worn backward, was his younger brother.

Chechnya, where the brothers grew up, has been the scene of two wars between Russian forces and separatists since 1994, in which tens of thousands were killed in heavy Russian bombing. That spawned an Islamic insurgency that has carried out deadly bombings in Russia and the region, although not in the West.

The older brother had strong political views about the United States, said Albrecht Ammon, 18, a downstairs-apartment neighbor in Cambridge. Ammon quoted Tsarnaev as saying that the U.S. uses the Bible as "an excuse for invading other countries."

Also, the FBI interviewed the older brother at the request of a foreign government in 2011, and nothing derogatory was found, according to a federal law enforcement official who was not authorized to discuss the case publicly and spoke on condition of anonymity.

The official did not identify the foreign country or say why it made the request.

Exactly how the long night of crime began was unclear. But police said the brothers carjacked a man in a Mercedes-Benz in Cambridge, just across the Charles River from Boston, then released him unharmed at a gas station.

They also shot to death a Massachusetts Institute of Technology police officer, 26-year-old Sean Collier, while he was responding to a report of a disturbance, investigators said.

The search for the Mercedes led to a chase that ended in Watertown, where authorities said the suspects threw explosive devices from the car and exchanged gunfire with police. A transit police officer, 33-year-old Richard Donohue, was shot and critically wounded, authorities said.

A man applauds as police leave the scene of the arrest of a suspect of the Boston Marathon bombings in Watertown, April 19, 2013. (AP Photo/Charles Krupa)

Dzhokhar Tsarnaev ran over his already wounded brother as he fled, according to two law enforcement officials who spoke on condition of anonymity because they were not authorized to discuss the investigation. At some point, he abandoned his car and ran away on foot.

The brothers had built an arsenal of pipe bombs, grenades and improvised explosive devices and used some of the weapons in trying to make their getaway, said Rep. Dutch Ruppersberger, D-Md., a member of the House Intelligence Committee.

Watertown resident Kayla Dipaolo said she was woken up overnight by gunfire and a large explosion that sounded "like it was right next to my head ... and shook the whole house."

"It was very scary," she said. "There are two bullet holes in the side of my house, and by the front door there is another."

Tamerlan Tsarnaev had studied accounting as a part-time student at Bunker Hill Community College in Boston for three semesters from 2006 to 2008, the school said.

Dzhokhar Tsarnaev was registered as a student at the University of Massachusetts Dartmouth. Students said he was on campus this week after the Boston Marathon bombing. The campus closed down Friday along with colleges around the Boston area.

The men's father, Anzor Tsarnaev, said in a telephone interview with AP from the Russian city of Makhachkala that his younger son, Dzhokhar, is "a true angel." He said his son was studying medicine.

"He is such an intelligent boy," the father said. "We expected him to come on holidays here."

A man who said he knew Dzhokhar Tsarnaev and Krystle Campbell, the 29-year-old restaurant manager killed in Monday's bombing, said he was glad Dzhokhar had survived.

"I didn't want to lose more than one friend," Marvin Salazar said.

"Why Jahar?" he asked, using Tsarnaev's nickname. "I want to know answers. That's the most important thing. And I think I speak for almost all America. Why the Boston Marathon? Why this year? Why Jahar?"

Two years ago, the city of Cambridge awarded Dzhokhar Tsarnaev a $2,500 scholarship. At the time, he was a senior at Cambridge Rindge & Latin School, a highly regarded public school whose alumni include Matt Damon, Ben Affleck and NBA Hall of Famer Patrick Ewing.

Tsarni, the men's uncle, said the brothers traveled here together from Russia. He called his nephews "losers" and said they had struggled to settle in the U.S. and ended up "thereby just hating everyone."

BOSTON BOMB SUSPECT HOSPITALIZED UNDER HEAVY GUARD
April 21, 2013
By Bridget Murphy and Katie Zezima

Boston Marathon bombing suspect Dzhokhar Tsarnaev lay hospitalized in serious condition under heavy guard Saturday (April 20) apparently in no shape to be interrogated as investigators tried to establish the motive for the deadly attack and the scope of the plot.

People across the Boston area breathed easier the morning after Tsarnaev, 19, was pulled, wounded and bloody, from a tarp-covered boat in a Watertown backyard. The capture came at the end of a tense day that began with his 26-year-old brother, Tamerlan, dying in a gun battle with police.

There was no immediate word on when Tsarnaev might be charged and what those charges would be. The twin bombings killed three people and wounded more than 180.

Police stand guard outside Beth Israel Deaconess Medical Center after an ambulance carrying Dzhokhar Tsarnaev arrived. Tsarnaev is hospitalized in serious condition with unspecified injuries after he was captured in an all-day manhunt, April 19, 2013. (AP Photo/Elise Amendola)

The most serious charge available to federal prosecutors would be the use of a weapon of mass destruction to kill people, which carries a possible death sentence. Massachusetts does not have the death penalty.

President Barack Obama said there are many unanswered questions about the bombing, including whether the Tsarnaev brothers ethnic Chechens from southern Russia who had been in the U.S. for about a decade and lived in the Boston area had help from others. The president urged people not to rush judgment about their motivations.

U.S. officials said an elite interrogation team would question the Massachusetts college student without reading him his Miranda rights, something that is allowed on a limited basis when the public may be in immediate danger, such as instances in which bombs are planted and ready to go off.

The American Civil Liberties Union expressed concern about that possibility. Executive Director Anthony Romero said the legal exception applies only when there is a continued threat to public safety and is "not an open-ended exception" to the Miranda rule, which guarantees the right to remain silent and the right to an attorney.

The federal public defender's office in Massachusetts said it has agreed to represent Tsarnaev once he is charged. Miriam Conrad, public defender for Massachusetts, said he should have a lawyer appointed as soon as possible because there are "serious issues regarding possible interrogation."

Massachusetts Gov. Deval Patrick said Saturday afternoon that Tsarnaev was in serious but stable condition and was probably unable to communicate. Tsarnaev was at Boston's Beth Israel Deaconess Medical Center, where 11 victims of the bombing were still being treated.

"I, and I think all of the law enforcement officials, are hoping for a host of reasons the suspect survives," the governor said after a ceremony at Fenway Park to honor the victims and survivors of the attack. "We have a million questions, and those questions need to be answered."

The all-day manhunt Friday brought the Boston area to a near standstill and put people on edge across the metropolitan area.

The break came around nightfall when a homeowner in Watertown saw blood on his boat, pulled back the tarp and saw a bloody Dzhokhar Tsarnaev hiding inside, police said. After an exchange of gunfire, he was seized and taken away in an ambulance.

Raucous celebrations erupted in and around Boston, with chants of "USA! USA!" Residents flooded the streets in relief four days after the two pressure-cooker bombs packed with nails and other shrapnel went off.

Michael Spellman said he bought tickets to Saturday's Red Sox game at Fenway Park to help send a message to the bombers.

"They're not going to stop us from doing things we love to do," he said, sitting a few rows behind home plate. "We're not going to live in fear."

During the long night of violence leading up to the capture, the Tsarnaev brothers killed an MIT police officer, severely wounded another lawman and took part in a furious shootout and car chase in which they hurled explosives at police from a large homemade arsenal, authorities said.

"We're in a gunfight, a serious gunfight. Rounds are going and then all of the sudden they see something being thrown at them and there's a huge explosion," Watertown Police Chief Edward Deveau said Saturday of the melee.

The chief said one of the explosives was the same type used during the Boston Marathon attack, and authorities later recovered a pressure cooker lid that had embedded in a car down the street. He said the suspects also tossed two grenades before Tamerlan ran out of ammunition and police tackled him.

But while handcuffing him, officers had to dive out of the way as Dzhokhar drove the carjacked Mercedes at them, Deveau said. The sport utility vehicle dragged Tamerlan's body down the block, he said. Police initially tracked the escaped suspect by a blood trail he left behind a house after abandoning the Mercedes, negotiating his surrender hours later after an area resident saw blood and found the suspect huddled in his boat.

Chechnya, where the Tsarnaev family has roots, has been the scene of two wars between Russian forces and separatists since 1994. That spawned an Islamic insurgency that has carried out deadly bombings in Russia and the region, although not in the West.

Investigators have not offered a motive for the Boston attack. But in interviews with officials and those who knew the Tsarnaevs, a picture has emerged of the older one as someone embittered toward the U.S., increasingly vehement in his Muslim faith and influential over his younger brother.

The Russian FSB intelligence service told the FBI in 2011 about information that Tamerlan Tsarnaev was a follower of radical Islam, two law enforcement officials said Saturday.

According to an FBI news release, a foreign government said that Tamerlan Tsarnaev appeared to be strong believer and that he had changed drastically since 2010 as he prepared to leave the U.S. for travel to the Russian region to join unspecified underground groups.

The FBI did not name the foreign government, but the two officials said it was Russia. The officials spoke on condition of anonymity because they were not authorized to talk about the matter publicly.

The FBI said that in response, it interviewed Tamerlan Tsarnaev and relatives, and did not find any domestic or foreign terrorism activity. The bureau said it looked into such things as his telephone and online activity, his travels and his associations with others.

Vehicles are parked at the Devens Federal Medical Center (FMC) in Devens, Mass. The U.S. Marshals Service said that Dzhokhar Tsarnaev had been moved from a Boston hospital to the federal medical center at Devens, about 40 miles west of the city, April 26, 2013. (AP Photo/Elise Amendola)

An uncle of the Tsarnaev brothers said he had a falling-out with Tamerlan over the man's increased commitment to Islam.

Ruslan Tsarni of Montgomery Village, Md., said Tamerlan told him in a 2009 phone conversation that he had chosen "God's business" over work or school. Tsarni said he then contacted a family friend who told him Tsarnaev had been influenced by a recent convert to Islam.

Sean Collier said his relationship with his nephew basically ended after that call.

As for Dzhokhar Tsarnaev, "he's been absolutely wasted by his older brother. I mean, he used him. He used him for whatever he's done," Tsarni said.

Albrecht Ammon, a downstairs-apartment neighbor of Tamerlan Tsarnaev in Cambridge, said in an interview that the older brother had strong political views about the United States. Ammon quoted Tsarnaev as saying that the U.S. uses the Bible as "an excuse for invading other countries."

Tamerlan Tsarnaev studied accounting as a part-time student at Bunker Hill Community College in Boston for three semesters from 2006 to 2008, the school said. He was married with a young daughter. Dzhokhar Tsarnaev was a student at the University of Massachusetts Dartmouth.

As of Saturday, more than 50 victims of the bombing remained hospitalized, three in critical condition.

PHOTOS FORCE SUSPECTS' MOVE, BREAKING BOMBING CASE
April 19, 2013
By Adam Geller

Moments after investigators went before television cameras to broadcast photos of the two men in ball caps wanted for the Boston Marathon bombing, queries from viewers started cascading in 300,000 hits a minute that overwhelmed the FBI's website.

Police in tactical gear arrive on an armored police vehicle as they surround an apartment building while looking for a suspect in the Boston Marathon bombings in Watertown, April 19, 2013. (AP Photo/Charles Krupa)

It marked a key turning point in a search that, for all the intensity of its first 72 hours, had failed to locate the suspects. While it's unclear how much the tips that resulted helped investigators zero in, experts say it instantly turned up already intense pressure on the two men to flee or almost certainly be recognized increasing the chances they'd make mistakes that would lead to them being exposed.

The decision to ask the public for help also was something of a gamble, one that investigators had to weigh carefully.

"It was a good decision to put this out to the public....and this would have been a calculated risk. But the intent would have been to get these guys to change their pattern" of behavior, said Martin Reardon, who spent 21 years as an FBI agent and is now a vice president of security consultant The Soufan Group.

Releasing the photos greatly increased the odds the two men would be recognized and turned in, even as it significantly upped the chances they would try to vanish or commit more mayhem exactly the scenario that has played out.

"Clearly these guys were reacting and responding exactly as (law enforcement) predicted," said Robert Taylor, a criminologist at the University of Texas at Dallas who studies terrorism. "If you saw your face on TV and everywhere else as associated with the bombing ... you would act irrationally and that's exactly what they did."

After three days without being able to identify a suspect by name, investigators clearly made the decision to release the photos Thursday on the belief that, without doing so, the suspects might remain at-large for weeks or months, with the chance to flee or to act again, said David Weinstein, a former federal prosecutor in Miami.

So with photos in hand, investigators made a choice deemed both necessary and prudent.

"And then the worst possible thing happens," Weinstein said. "They do actually begin their flight and then start to wreak vengeance on the whole city of Boston."

Weinstein, Reardon and other experts had differing opinions on whether investigators' decision to release the photos was worth the cost exacted by the two men: the killing of a Massachusetts Institute of Technology police officer, a carjacking, the shooting of another transit police officer and a block-by-block manhunt that led officials to shut Boston and many of its surrounding suburbs.

But all agreed the photo release was pivotal in breaking open the case, because it instantly deprived suspected bombers Tamerlan Tsarnaev, 26, and his 19-year-old brother, Dzhokhar, of time, anonymity and options.

A SWAT team marches through a neighborhood while searching for a suspect in Watertown, Mass., April 19, 2013. (AP Photo/Charles Krupa)

By late Friday (April 19), many of the details in the chain of events that led to the older brother's death and a massive hunt for the younger one were still unclear, but the pursuit had consumed the region with apprehension, tempered by hope that it might be nearing an end.

It began just after 5 p.m. Thursday, when investigators released the photographs and video of two unidentified suspects and asked for the public's help. Just over five hours later, shots were heard on the campus of the Massachusetts Institute of Technology, across the Charles River from Boston in Cambridge. Ten minutes later, an MIT campus police officer who was responding was found shot multiple times in his vehicle and was later pronounced dead.

Soon after, two armed men carjacked a Mercedes SUV in Cambridge, holding the driver for about half an hour before releasing him unharmed. Police pursued and the men inside the vehicle threw explosive devices from the windows, while exchanging gunfire. A Massachusetts Bay Transportation Authority officer was wounded in a firefight with the suspects and the older brother, Tamerlan Tsarnaev, was critically injured and pronounced dead.

The hunt then continued for the younger brother, who fled on foot.

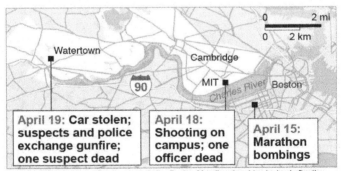

Boston police say one of two suspects in the Boston Marathon bombing is dead after the killing of an MIT police officer and a shootout with police. A massive manhunt is underway for the other.

This locator map shows the location and time line of the suspects in the Boston Marathon explosions, April 19, 2013. (AP Photo)

In the pre-dawn hours Friday, dozens of police officer and FBI agents converged on Watertown, Mass. after gunshots and explosions were heard, ordering people to stay inside. But the search proved fruitless, leading authorities to shut down Boston's mass transit system and urge residents of several cities and towns to stay indoors.

State Police spokesman Dave Procopio said police realized they were dealing with the bombing suspects based on what the two men told the carjacking victim during their getaway attempt.

"We believe this man to be a terrorist," Boston Police Commissioner Ed Davis said, of the brother who remained a fugitive late Friday. "We believe this to be a man who's come here to kill people."

The chaos of the pursuit contrasted sharply with the sweeping, methodical investigation that began almost immediately after the Monday afternoon bombing that killed three and wounded more than 180, marked by officials' notable reluctance to disclose information. In the hours and days immediately after the bombing, dozens of investigators in white hooded suits carefully combed, cataloged and photographed evidence at the scene, even canvassing the roofs of nearby buildings to search for items blown into the air by the bomb's force.

Investigators gathered hours of videotape footage from security cameras that scanned the area around the bombing and appealed to the public to turn in their own video and photos, for help in determining the sequence of events and identifying a suspect.

The investigation will probably collect about a million hours of videotape from fixed security cameras and spectators' cellphones and cameras, said Gene Grindstaff, a scientist at Intergraph Corp., a company that makes video analysis software used by the FBI and other law enforcement agencies.

Investigators used software to search for certain types of objects or people matching a height and weight description. The software can also spot patterns that human analysts might not notice, such as a car that turns up in different places, he said.

"Back in the days of 20 years ago, you were lucky if you had video and it was probably of poor quality and it took a tremendous amount of enhancement. Today you have a completely different issue," Grindstaff said.

"Here's the first thing that the computer was told: Tell me if you can find the same people at both of those (bombing) locations," said Taylor, the criminologist.

A crowd gathers at Boston Common after the final suspect in the Boston Marathon bombing was arrested, April 19, 2013. (AP Photo/Julio Cortez)

Additional parameters would further narrow the search to, for example, look for people carrying backpacks.

"It's kind of like going through a series of strainers and filters," Taylor said.

But with the video winnowed down, the process required examination frame-by-frame, a laborious process done by an FBI unit called the Operational Technologies Division, said Joe DiZinno, former director of the FBI lab in Virginia.

By Thursday, once facial recognition software and agents had narrowed the search to images of two young men, investigators had to make a decision about how to proceed.

Meanwhile, the Tsarnaev brothers were already on edge.

At an auto body shop near their home, the younger brother, Dzhokhar, had often stopped to talk with owner Gilberto Junior about cars and soccer. But on Tuesday, the day after the bombing, the normally relaxed young man showed up biting his nails and trembling, Junior said.

The mechanic told Tsarnaev he hadn't had a chance to work on a Mercedes he'd dropped off for bumper work.

"I don't care. I don't care. I need the car right now," Junior says Dzhokhar Tsarnaev told him.

By Thursday afternoon, the brothers had to know their options were narrowing quickly. And then the FBI released their photos to millions of viewers across the city, and around the world via newspaper, television stations and websites. The time to move was now.

"I think this developed rather quickly last night," State Police Col. Timothy Alben said late Friday. "I would wager that most of the activity that was printed in the media yesterday forced them to make decisions or take actions that ultimately revealed who they were."

3

AFTERMATH

Running shoes hang from a makeshift memorial in Copley Square on Boylston Street in Boston, April 24, 2013. (AP Photo/Michael Dwyer)

DEFIANCE, TENDERNESS, WARINESS IN WAKE OF BOSTON
April 17, 2013
By Nancy Benac

A Virginia woman makes a point to get out and go jogging. A Texas mom stays in and snuggles her toddler a little closer. A nurse from Massachusetts looks over her shoulder more often while touring D.C.

Strains of defiance, tenderness and wariness are interwoven as Americans are forced to do some post-9-11 rebalancing in the aftermath of the Boston bombings, figuring out how to move forward with life while remaining vigilant against the threat of terrorism.

The discovery of tainted letters sent to the Capitol and the White House only added a new source of jitters to the week's events, evoking eerie parallels to the anthrax attacks that followed the life-altering events of Sept. 11, 2001.

For Simone Rinaldi, playing tourist in Washington this week with her family, the twin bombings at the marathon quickly revived thoughts of the collapse of the Twin Towers in New York as she wondered anew if there would be other attacks and whether loved ones in Boston were safe.

"I've definitely been more cautious as we walk around," said Rinaldi, a nurse practitioner from Cape Cod, Mass.

Cautious, yes. But not cowed.

Marathon runner Benton Berman accompanied by his dog Tank pauses on Boylston Street near the finish line, April 17, 2013. (AP Photo/Matt Rourke)

"The world is a really scary place, yet we have a life to live," she said from a park across Pennsylvania Avenue from the White House. "The challenge is to take precautions, but again to not let our lives get small and live in fear."

Similar sentiment echoed around the country from a Starbucks table in Los Angeles to a smoker's bench in Billings, Mont. as people grappled with the balancing act involved in putting the week's events in perspective.

"Caution is always important, but so is life," said MacKenzie Edwins, a receptionist catching lunch at the Starbucks in LA.

Jennifer Miller, a hospitality industry manager smoking a cigarette on that bench in Montana, said the marathon bombing made her think this: "It's at home in America. It happened here." But also this: "I refuse to live in fear of going anywhere or doing anything."

Such perspective is precisely what terrorists try to destroy, by provoking reactions far out of proportion to actual danger.

Horrific as the bombing was three people died in Boston, with more than 170 injured five people die in car, truck or motorcycle accidents every hour in the U.S. Terrorism pushes our fear buttons, says security expert Bruce Schneier, and we have an outsized response.

"Psychologically, we are primed to overreact," he says.

And that can cause people to surrender civil liberties without full deliberation in pursuit of safety and stronger law enforcement, as happened after 9-11, Schneier warns: "The fear is that this is an excuse to put us into a police state."

Around the country, people wondered whether the bombing would and should affect security restrictions.

Security may increase for a time, but "the sad thing is it always goes back to normal," said Lynn Chamberlain, a training coordinator at Johns Hopkins Medicine in Baltimore.

"Now we're going to have to raise up not only our national security but our local security," said Zeke Reardon, a Denver electrician.

Terrorism peaked as a public concern just one month after the 9/11 attacks. In October 2001, Gallup found that 46 percent of Americans called terrorism the most important problem facing the country, up from less than 1 percent in the days before the attack.

It has not reached that level of importance since, and in surveys this year, it once again stood at less than 1 percent.

But while it may not be Issue No. 1, security nonetheless remains a priority for most Americans. In a January 2013 poll by the Pew Research Center, 71 percent said defending against terrorism should be a top priority for the president and Congress, down just 5 points from four years earlier.

In Seattle, accountant John Calhoun laments that young people may be desensitized to the threat of terrorism in the post-9-11 environment. He was troubled that his children, ages 13 and 21, weren't more upset as they watched news about the marathon bombing unfold on TV.

"It's a different world than we used to think we lived in," Calhoun said, wearing a half-marathon shirt from a past race as he ran stairs at the Seattle Art Museum's Olympic Sculpture Park on a sunny Tuesday afternoon.

Runners, in particular, seemed to push back against the notion that the marathon bombing could intimidate Americans.

Spontaneous running events popped up around the country, and social media was filled with posts from those pulling on their sneakers to send a message.

"I am going running today as a small sign of support for Boston and to show those responsible for the tragic events that we are stronger than they are," Ironman CEO Andrew Messick said in an email to athletes.

Two young boys leave messages with chalk on a sidewalk near the finish line, April 18, 2013. (AP Photo/Matt Rourke)

Tammi DeVan, in Alexandria, Va., did just that. "Jogged a couple miles for those who will never be able to again," she posted on Facebook.

For some Americans, the bombing was reason to slow down at least for a moment, and to hope it would bring Americans closer together.

"Usually at this time of day, I am looking for an excuse to get out of my house," Nancy Worth, a mother of four in Plano, Texas, posted on Facebook on Tuesday. "Today I feel happy to stay home, do mundane things like laundry, and snuggle Sammy," her 2-year-old.

Ed Starbuck scrubs on his 5-year-old beagle, Rosie, as they stand vigil at a makeshift memorial to the Boston Marathon, April 18, 2013. (AP Photo/Allen Breed)

"What's important right now is that it brings us closer together in times of tragedy," said Kathryn King, a Baltimore pediatrician who grew up not far from where the Virginia Tech shootings unfolded six years ago. The Boston bombings reminded her of how her neighbors in Virginia "taught the nation how it is to stand together and heal."

There may be a lesson for all Americans in the reaction of those injured in the Boston bombings.

Dr. Horacio Hojman, associate chief of trauma at Tufts Medical Center, which treated some of the injured, said that despite the seriousness of their injuries, patients were in surprisingly good spirits when they were brought in.

"Despite what they witnessed, despite what they suffered, despite many of them having life-threatening injuries, their spirits were not broken," he said. "And I think that should probably be the message for all of us that this horrible act of terror will not bring us down, and I think that the patients were the ones who say that the loudest."

David Lee, a truck driver from Lansing, Mich., gave voice to both that unbroken spirit and the worries that nag at Americans as they grapple with an unknown source of the terror.

"They want everyone to alter their lives again. And I said to myself, `Well, I'm not going to get all wrapped up in this,'" Lee said.

But he also allowed: "When you're alone at night, in the dark, it worries you. It affects you. You think about the people that someone thought were expendable for them to get their point across."

ANGER, FEAR, TEARS NORMAL
RESPONSE TO DISASTERS
April 19, 2013
By Lauran Neergaard and Carla K. Johnson

Kaitlyn Greeley burst into tears when a car backfired the other day. She's afraid to take her usual train to her job at a Boston hospital, walking or taking cabs instead. She can't sleep.

"I know this is how people live every day in other countries. But I'm not used to it here," said Greeley, 27, a technician at Tufts Medical Center who was on duty Monday when part of the hospital was briefly evacuated even as victims of the blast were being treated in the emergency room.

Anger, crying jags and nightmares are all normal reactions for both survivors of the Boston Marathon bombings and witnesses to the mayhem. While the injured and those closest to the blasts are most prone to psychological aftershocks, even people with no physical injuries and those like Greeley might feel the emotional impact for weeks afterward as they struggle to regain a sense of security. What's not clear is who will suffer lingering anxiety, depression or even post-traumatic stress disorder.

But specialists say that how resilient people are helps determine how quickly they bounce back. The resilient tend to be people who share their emotions before becoming overwhelmed, who know how to cope with stress, and who have the ability to look for a silver lining such as focusing on bystanders who helped the wounded.

Focusing on the horror, "that's harder on our body and our mind," said Dr. Catherine Mogil, co-director of the family trauma service at the University of California, Los Angeles. "People who tend to be able to make positive meaning out of tough situations are going to fare better."

Emma MacDonald, 21, center, cries during a vigil for the victims of the Boston Marathon explosions at Boston Common, April 16, 2013. (AP Photo/Julio Cortez)

Among the typical reactions that psychologists say anyone who witnessed the bombings or their aftermath might experience include difficulty sleeping or eating; sweats or stomachaches; anxiety or fear especially in crowded situations that remind people of the bombing. People may have a hard time focusing on work or other everyday activities. They may feel numb, anger easily, or cry often.

Priscilla Dass-Brailsford, a psychologist at Georgetown University Medical Center, said that if those symptoms don't fade in about a month, of if they are bad enough to impair function, people should seek help.

But for most, "time is a great healer," said Dass-Brailsford, who served on disaster mental health teams that counseled survivors of 9/11 in New York.

Specialists say only a small number of people are expected to be so severely affected that they develop PTSD, a disorder that can include flashbacks, debilitating anxiety, irritability and insomnia months after the trauma. Even among veterans of the Iraq and Afghanistan wars, the best estimate was that just under 20 percent returned with symptoms of PTSD or major depression.

More at risk for lingering psychological effects are people who've previously been exposed to trauma, whether from the battlefield, a car crash or a hurricane.

During two stints in Iraq as a Marine, Eusebio Collazo of Humble, Texas, was gravely wounded and today runs regularly to help deal with PTSD. Running with a veterans group called Team Red, White & Blue, he was at mile 25 of the marathon when the bombs detonated and adrenaline fueled his frantic race to find his wife, Karla, at the finish line. She was unharmed.

Lt. Mike Murphy of the Newton, Mass., fire dept., carries an American flag down the middle of Boylston Street after observing a moment of silence in honor of the victims of the bombing near the race finish line. At 2:50 p.m., exactly one week after the bombings, many bowed their heads and cried at the makeshift memorial on Boylston Street, three blocks from the site of the explosions, where bouquets of flowers, handwritten messages, and used running shoes were piled on the sidewalk, April 22, 2013. (AP Photo/Robert F. Bukaty)

"My wife keeps asking me, `I don't know how I should be feeling. I want to cry but I can't.' And then I want to cry, and I can't cry either. So, there's a lot of weird, different feelings going on," Collazo said Thursday. It's harder, he said, to handle explosions on the home front than in a war zone.

In Boston's hospitals, teams of counselors and social workers are telling patients and their families what to expect in the difficult days and weeks ahead.

"Most people are having a lot of flashbacks," and thoughts of the bombing interrupt their days and nights, said Lisa Allee, who directs the Community Violence Response Team at Boston Medical Center. "These are very typical, normal, expected emotions after any traumatic event or disaster."

Beyond hospitalized patients, part of coping is awareness about how to take care of the psyche turning off scary TV coverage and reading a book, going out for a quiet dinner, anything to temporarily cut the stress, says Dass-Brailsford, the disaster specialist.

That's especially true for parents who are trying to calm their children, added UCLA's Mogil, because kids take their emotional cues from the adults around them. Younger children especially don't need to see repeated footage of the blasts, because they may think it's happening again.

For a lot of people, psychiatrists say, talking about their experience can be cathartic.

A cashier's routine "how are you?" was enough for Anndee Hochman to tear up in a Philadelphia hardware store Wednesday. Hochman and her 12-year-old daughter had traveled to Boston to watch her partner run the marathon and all three were in different places when the bombs exploded, Hochman herself just a few blocks from the finish line.

Hochman spent 10 minutes telling the store clerk her family's story of reuniting and said it helps every time she's told friends, family, even a near-stranger about the experience.

Unknowingly, Hochman echoed the advice to look for a silver lining as she counseled daughter Sasha, who was nervous about returning to school.

"I reminded her, " `Sweetie' and reminded myself, too `there may have been a few people who planned those bombs and wanted to hurt people," Hochman said, "but there are so many more people there and in the world who want to help.'"

PRESSURE COOKER BOMBS USED IN PAST BY MILITANTS
April 16, 2013
By Lee Keath

Homemade bombs built from pressure cookers, a version of which was used in the Boston Marathon bombings, have been a frequent weapon of militants in Afghanistan, India and Pakistan. Al-Qaida's branch in Yemen once published an online manual on how to make one, urging "lone jihadis" to act on their own to carry out attacks.

President Barack Obama underlined Tuesday (April 16) that investigators do not know if the twin bombing the day before that killed three people and wounded more than 170 was carried out by an international organization, a domestic group or a "malevolent individual." There has been no claim of responsibility.

Investigators comb through the post finish line area of the Boston Marathon at Boylston Street. Authorities investigating the deadly bombings have recovered a piece of circuit board that they believe was part of one of the explosive devices, and also found the lid of a pressure cooker that apparently was catapulted onto the roof of a nearby building, April 17, 2013. (AP Photo/Julio Cortez)

A person briefed on the investigation told The Associated Press that the explosives were fashioned out of pressure cookers and packed with shards of metal, nails and ball bearings to inflict maximum carnage.

The relative ease of constructing such bombs and the powerful punch they deliver has made them attractive to insurgents and Islamic extremists, particularly in South Asia. They have turned up in past bombing plots by Islamic extremists in the West, including a plan by a U.S. soldier to blow up a restaurant frequented by fellow soldiers outside Fort Hood, in Texas. One of the three devices used in the May 2010 Times Square attempted bombing was a pressure cooker, according to a joint FBI and Homeland Security intelligence report issued in July 2010.

Al-Qaida's branch in Yemen gave a detailed description on how to make a pressure cooker bomb in the 2010 first issue of "Inspire," its magazine that only appears online, in a chapter titled "Make a bomb in the kitchen of your mom."

"The pressurized cooker is the most effective method" for making a simple bomb, the article said, describing how to fill the cooker with shrapnel and gunpowder and to create a detonator using the filament of a light bulb and a clock timer.

"Inspire" magazine has a running series of such training articles called "Open Source Jihad," which the group calls a resource manual for individual extremists to carry out attacks against the enemies of jihad, including the U.S. and its allies. The magazine is targeted heavily at encouraging "lone wolf" jihadis.

An issue last year reprinted an older article by a veteran Syrian jihadi Abu Musab al-Souri addressing would-be jihadis proposing a long list of possible targets for attacks, among them "crowded sports arenas" and "annual social events."

Notably, Army Pfc. Naser Jason Abdo, who was convicted and sentenced to life in prison last year for the Fort Hood restaurant bombing plot, was discovered to have a copy of the "How to build a bomb in the kitchen of your mom" article, according to the FBI. Investigators found bomb making materials in his hotel that included a pressure cooker and gunpowder, according to testimony at his trial.

The SITE Monitoring Service, a U.S. independent group tracking militant messaging online, noted that Islamic extremists are not the only ones paying attention to the al-Qaida magazine: White supremacists have also circulated copies on their web forums. They found "Inspire" and "other al-Qaida manuals beneficial for their strategies," it said.

Over the course of 10 issues the past three years, "Inspire" has given detailed instructions with diagrams and photos on how to use automatic weapons, produce remote control detonators, set fire to a building or create forest fires. In the most recent issue, put out in March, it described how to set fire to a parked vehicle and how to cause road accidents with oil slicks on a road or tire-bursting spikes.

A portion of a pressure-cooker bomb recovered from a blast site at the Boston Marathon bombing is displayed for the media in a conference room after the conclusion of the day's session at the Dzhokhar Tsarnaev federal death penalty trial at the John Joseph Moakley United States Courthouse in Boston, March 11, 2015. (AP Photo/Charles Krupa)

The chapters, including the one on pressure cooker bombs, were compiled into a booklet titled "The Lone Mujahed Pocket-book," released on Islamic militant web sites in March, according to SITE.

Al-Qaida's Yemeni branch, known as al-Qaida in the Arabian Peninsula, has repeatedly tried to carry out direct attacks on U.S. soil, once by dispatching the would-be 2009 Christmas bomber of a U.S. jet whose attack failed when the explosives hidden in his underwear failed to go off and then the following year by trying to mail explosives to the U.S. in packages that were intercepted.

The pressure cooker bomb's most frequent use seems to be in Afghanistan, Pakistan, Nepal and India in attacks against police or the public. This year, local press reports in Pakistan have reported several such bombs found planted on streets, including in the city of Karachi, where multiple militant groups operate.

In 2010, suspected militants attacked the U.S.-based Christian aid group World Vision in northwestern Pakistan, killing six Pakistani employees with a remotely detonated pressure cooker bomb.

That same year, the U.S. Department of Homeland Security put out a warning about such explosives, noting their frequent use in South Asia.

"The presence of a pressure cooker in an unusual location such as a building lobby or busy street corner should be treated as suspicious," it said.

MARATHON OFFICIALS KNOW BETTER
SECURITY DIFFICULT
April 17, 2013
By Howard Fendrich

A marathon course runs 26.2 miles along an open road. Much tougher to secure than an arena with doors and walls.

Yet across the U.S. and around the world, from West Bend, Wis., and London this weekend, to Nashville, Tenn., next week and Copenhagen next month, organizers of road races are trying to figure out how to improve security after the Boston Marathon bombings.

Paris Marathon director Joel Laine, whose race was held earlier this month, put it this way Tuesday (April 16): "There will be a `before' and `after-Boston'" from now on.

Still, with thousands and sometimes hundreds of thousands of spectators and entrants scattered along the route, there are limits to how much can be done to protect everyone, marathon officials, experts and runners cautioned. They spoke in dozens of interviews with the AP a day after a pair of bombs went off seconds apart near the finish line in Boston, killing three people, including an 8-year-old boy, and injuring more than 170 others.

"This is what everyone thought might happen" following the 9/11 attacks, said Tom Derderian, coach of the Greater Boston Track Club and author of a book about the Boston Marathon.

"This is a 26-mile foot race. With both sides of the street, that's 52 miles to secure," Derderian said. "How? You can't have everyone go through metal detectors."

Marathons aren't just for elite athletes: They have steadily increased in popularity among recreational runners and those raising money for charity. In the aftermath of Monday's attack, which President Barack Obama called an act of terrorism, some marathons heard from runners wondering whether races would be canceled. Yet nearly 40 events, all over the globe, are set for this weekend alone including Hamburg, Belgrade, Salt Lake City, Lansing, Mich., and the Jersey Shore. There was no indication that any would be called off.

Security personnel stand guard behind spectators as they watch the Pittsburgh Marathon, May 5, 2013. (AP Photo/Keith Srakocic)

Scott Dickey, CEO of Competitor Group Inc., which manages more than 35 marathons and half marathons around the world, said he's "been in deep conversations already" with the FBI and government agencies "to talk about enhancing security protocol and personnel" for the St. Jude Country Music Marathon and Half Marathon in Nashville on April 27.

"What we're going to do with yesterday's event is we're going to learn from it, and we're going to increase, certainly in the near term and probably permanently, the number of security personnel, both private and public, at our start lines and finish lines," Dickey said. "We're going to review the protocol and procedures that are in place and enhance and improve them so that we're in a better position to prevent these types of tragedies from taking place."

Susie Smisek, director of September's Omaha Marathon, said Boston does, indeed, change the way race organizers go about their job now.

"We'll make sure we have more security available, that people are more aware and are aware of their surroundings," Smisek said. "Will it make us more vigilant in what we do? You bet."

Rick Nealis, director of the Marine Corps Marathon since 1993, pointed to factors that make these races unique among sports and, therefore, more of a challenge to secure.

"It's a participatory sport. At any running event, especially Boston, world champion and Olympic athletes stand at the start line, and at the same time, there's someone from Boise, Idaho, or Duluth, Minn., that did the qualifying time and are in the same field, on the same course, in the same weather as these champions, competing," Nealis said.

"In stadiums, turnstiles, hardened buildings, you can control who's going in, and do all the safety checks and have a secure event," added Nealis, whose race course cuts through Virginia and the nation's capital, ending near the Iwo Jima Memorial. "On roads, in an open venue, when you take 26.2 miles of open space, it's the beauty of the sport and at the same time, in this day and age, part of the risk assessment. Unless we decide we're going to run around a track in quarter-mile loops hundreds of times."

The New York City Marathon's finishers grew from nearly 28,000 in 1992 to more than 47,000 in 2011, and organizers estimate they've had as many as roughly 2 million spectators in a year. The race was not held in 2012, after Superstorm Sandy hit the area, but Mayor Michael Bloomberg said Tuesday: "It's certainly our intention to have the marathon" this November.

"A marathon is 26 miles long, so, you know, there are points of vulnerability by definition, there are going to be," New York City Police Commissioner Raymond Kelly said, noting the race's security plans will be reevaluated.

According to Running USA's website, a record 30 marathons had more than 10,000 finishers in 2012, led by Chicago with more than 37,000, followed by London with more than 36,000.

The Honolulu Marathon ranked seventh on that list with just over 24,000.

"You can't plan to stop everything, but certainly everyone will look at tightening things up, for sure. You have to strike some balances between what is feasible and what is possible and what is necessary," said Jim Barahal, president of December's Honolulu race. "It's going to have effects outside the marathon world, which in reality is a pretty low-profile world. It can happen anywhere, at any time."

Dorte Vibjerg, organizer of the Copenhagen Marathon, said "the incident in Boston means we will have more focus on security."

"We can never prevent anything from happening," she said, "but we can minimize and react fast should anything happen."

Lefteris Plakidas, a spokesman for the association organizing Sunday's Alexander the Great Marathon in Thessaloniki, Greece, voiced the thoughts of organizers of various races around the world when responding to a question about whether fail-safe security measures can be implemented: "It is neither possible, nor does it make any sense in Greece. Just think, in our marathon, (half goes) through an industrial area. It's not possible to secure an area like this."

Security and bomb-sniffing dogs keep watch near the finish line of the 2013 New York City Marathon in New York, November 3, 2013. (AP Photo/Seth Wenig)

"But who could have imagined a terrorist attack at a marathon," Plakidas added, "a race of mass sport that is open to everyone, from athletes, children, older people, to people with special needs?"

That association's general secretary, Yiannis Podiotis, said the group spoke to local police after Monday's bombing, but there are limits to what can be done.

"What can we do, have 10,000 police running behind the runners?" Podiotis asked.

About 2,000 runners are expected for Sunday's marathon and 5-kilometer and 10-kilometer events there.

Gold Coast Marathon head Cameron Hart, whose race is expected to attract 30,000 runners in July, acknowledged that the attack in Boston raises concerns.

"The very fabric of having the runners go past public areas," Hart said, "means it's something that is impossible to lock down."

Akira Kazama, general secretary of Japan's track and field federation, said officials will beef up safety measures if needed.

Security at the starting area and the finish line are particularly tight, Kazama said, because only registered staff and runners are allowed. Security personnel stand along the course, facing the road, to try to quickly detect anything suspicious.

If security becomes more stringent, Kazama said, "the nice, peaceful atmosphere may be lost. That's unfortunate."

Lou Marciani, director of the National Center for Spectator Sports Safety and Security at The University of Southern Mississippi, said there has been a lot of progress since 9/11 especially when working to secure stadiums. But large, public events are especially vulnerable. He said the international flavor of the Boston Marathon could have been a factor in its appeal to the attackers.

"It's very logical," Marciani said. "If you're going to do something evil, and you can't get into something like a stadium, you're going to think outside the box. They went for the soft target."

Marciani expects tighter security at all major sporting events in the coming months and, yes, there were increased police at baseball stadiums and NHL arenas by Monday night but a targeted plan won't be developed until a full report comes from Boston.

No matter what law enforcement determines about Boston, Marciani expects start and finish lines at marathons to get the heaviest attention.

That's going to be the case for the 275 or so runners who will participate in the Adrenaline Marathon and other races Sunday in West Bend, Wis., according to organizer Mary Simon. There will be more bag checks there, too. Simon was pleased to see about 20 additional runners register in the aftermath of Boston's bombing.

"One of the great things about these marathons is that they are free and are available to the public. That's why we have hundreds and thousands of people come out and watch them. I can't see how that is going to change. It's part of the whole ethos of what a mass-participation marathon is about," said Nick Bitel, chief executive of the London Marathon.

"What one has to do is make appropriate and reasonable security measures in light of the threats," he added, "and that's what we'll be doing on Sunday."

MARATHON RESCUER GETS ATTENTION FROM PRESS AND FBI
April 18, 2013
By Jeff Donn

Just about everyone you can imagine stopped by Carlos Luis Arredondo's little brick row house Wednesday (April 17) to hear what he had to say about the Boston Marathon bombing. Reporters flew in from as far away as Paris, friends and neighbors strolled in, even two FBI agents made a visit.

Virtually overnight, Arredondo has turned into a living reminder of both the horror and bravery witnessed in Monday's double bombing at the finish line of the race.

Arredondo, a peace activist and sometime cabbie and truck driver who was watching the race from the finish line, rushed into the mass of mangled humanity, where a dramatic Associated Press photo caught him pushing a wheelchair with a victim who lost most of his lower legs in the attack.

"I was in a state of shock briefly, and then I realized I needed to help," Arredondo said in an interview at his home in southwest Boston. He said he had skills needed because he is a Red Cross volunteer trained in first aid.

His cowboy hat and riveting comments to reporters, as well as the news photographs of him rescuing bombing victim Jeff Bauman

Jr., quickly made him something of a sensation. The stream of reporters looked for the drama in his story, and friends offered words of encouragement.

The FBI agents, Arredondo said, asked routine questions in search of mundane facts they hoped would help them solve the extraordinary crime. Could Arredondo and his wife, Melida, verbally retrace their footsteps during the race? Where precisely were they when the bombs went off? What did they see? What did they do?

After about 40 minutes of questions, the FBI agents left without talking to reporters. Arredondo said they told him they'd contact him again later. The agents referred reporters' questions to their office, where officials could not be reached for comment late Wednesday.

Arredondo said Boston police had already stopped by Tuesday and asked for some personal belongings on behalf of the FBI, which is running the investigation. He gave them the shoes, pants and T-shirt he wore at the race, as well as four photographs he took immediately after the attack.

He wasn't specific about what investigators hoped to discover from his clothing, saying only that they took some items "they need to evaluate."

Carlos Arredondo speaks to reporters outside his home in the Roslindale neighborhood of Boston. Arredondo, a peace activist, whose son was killed during the Iraq war, was near the explosions and assisted victims, April 17, 2013. (AP Photo/Josh Reynolds)

"We were very happy to help them in any way we can," he added, standing beside his wife.

Even before Monday, Arredondo, a U.S. citizen who emigrated from Costa Rica, had lived through more than his share of grief and time in the glare of public spotlight during his 52 years.

When, in 2004, several Marines came to his Florida home with news that his older son, Lance Cpl. Alexander Arredondo, had been killed by a sniper in Iraq, the distraught Arredondo smashed the windows of their van, climbed inside and set it on fire. The Marines pulled him out with serious burns, but he later said he set the fire by accident, not to end his own life.

In 2011, his younger son, Brian, long addicted and depressed over his brother's death, committed suicide. "We both refused to admit that we had mental problems," Carlos Arredondo said at the funeral. According to The Boston Globe, Carlos sought inpatient psychiatric treatment.

On Wednesday, reporters sat waiting on benches in a postage-stamp-size memorial garden with a plaque dedicated to his older son. An American flag fluttered in the breeze. Antiwar signs were piled against a fence nearby in this working-class neighborhood of triple-decker houses and towering trees bearing the first buds of spring.

Over the years, Arredondo has become involved in antiwar activism and veterans' groups, making him a figure already recognized by many in the Boston area. Now his face, intent on the rescue, is known around the world.

Arredondo, who says he went to the marathon to meet with a group of National Guardsmen and military families who were cheering the runners and handing out U.S. flags, spoke Wednesday in a jersey from last year's marathon. On his chest he wore two buttons, each with a photo of one of his sons. He said that two participants in this year's marathon had been taking part in memory of his sons.

Bauman Jr., the 27-year-old man pictured being pushed by Arredondo, had been at the race to cheer on his girlfriend.

"I just can't explain what's wrong with people today, to do this to people," his father, also named Jeff Bauman, wrote in a Facebook post this week. "I'm really starting to lose faith in our country."

People who know Arredondo said Wednesday that they were not surprised that he jumped in to help the marathon victims. "He's an incredible guy. He's been through a lot," said neighbor Andrew Burton. He said Arredondo has stayed very outgoing and caring toward others, despite his own ordeals.

"He just saw something that needed to be done, and he just did it," said Vietnam veteran Bob Funke, a friend who stopped by to visit. "He's just that kind of person."

However, Arredondo did admit to being unnerved by all the attention Wednesday. And he added that he was worried about his own safety and that of others "because we don't know who caused this terrorist attack."

4

THE BROTHERS TSARNAEV

Customers watch the news on TV screens at the Granary Tavern in Boston. Two suspects in the Boston Marathon bombing killed an MIT police officer, injured a transit officer in a firefight and threw explosive devices at police during their getaway attempt in a long night of violence that left one of them dead and another still at large, April 19, 2013. (AP Photo/Elise Amendola)

THE STORIES OF 2 BROTHERS SUSPECTED IN BOMBING
April 20, 2013
By Jeff Donn and Jocelyn Noveck

Tamerlan Tsarnaev was an amateur boxer with muscular arms and enough brio to arrive at a sparring session without protective gear. His younger brother Dzhokhar was popular in high school, won a city scholarship for college and liked to hang out with Russian friends off-campus.

Details of two lives, suddenly infamous, came to light Friday (April 19). Overnight, two men previously seen only in grainy camera images were revealed to be ethnic Chechen brothers suspected in a horrific act of terrorism. Tamerlan was dead; his 19-year-old brother would be captured after a furious manhunt that shut down much of Boston.

But the details of their lives shed precious little light on the most vexing question: Why would two brothers who came to America a decade ago turn on their adopted home with an attack on a cherished tradition, the Boston Marathon?

The Tsarnaev family arrived in the United States, seeking refuge from strife in their homeland. "Why people go to America? You know why," the father, Anzor Tsarnaev, said in an interview from Russia, where he lives now. "Our political system in Russia. Chechens were persecuted in Kyrgyzstan, they were problems." The family had moved from Kyrgyzstan to Dagestan, a predominantly Muslim republic in Russia's North Caucasus that has become an epicenter of the Islamic insurgency that spilled over from Chechnya.

The father set up as an auto mechanic, and the two boys (there were two sisters, too) went to school. Dzhokhar, at least, attended the Cambridge Rindge and Latin school, a prestigious public school just blocks from Harvard Yard.

From there, the boys' paths diverged somewhat at least for a while.

Tamerlan, who was 26 when he was killed overnight in a shootout, dropped out after studying accounting at Bunker Hill Community College for just three semesters.

"I don't have a single American friend. I don't understand them," he was quoted as saying in a photo package that appeared in a Boston University student magazine in 2010.

He identified himself then as a Muslim and said he did not drink or smoke: "God said no alcohol." He said he hoped to fight for the U.S. Olympic team and become a naturalized American.

As a boxer, he was known for his nerve. "He's a real cocky guy," said one trainer who worked with him, Kendrick Ball. He said the young man came to his first sparring session with no protective gear. "That's unheard of with boxing," Ball said. But he added: "In this sport, you've got to be sure of yourself, you know what I mean?"

More recently, Tamerlan married, with a young daughter became a more devout Muslim, according to his aunt, Maret

Tsarnaeva. She told reporters outside her Toronto home Friday that the older brother had taken to praying five times a day.

In 2011, the FBI interviewed Tamerlan at the behest of a foreign government, a federal law enforcement official said, speaking anonymously. The officials would not say what country made the request or why, but said that nothing derogatory was found.

Albrecht Ammon, 18, lived directly below the apartment of the two suspects. He said he recently saw Tamerlan in a pizzeria, where they argued about religion and U.S. foreign policy. He quoted Tsarnaev as saying that many U.S. wars are based on the Bible, which is used as "an excuse for invading other countries."

During the argument, Ammon said, Tsarnaev told him he had nothing against the American people, but he had something against the American government. "The Bible was a cheap copy of the Koran," Ammon quoted Tsarnaev as saying.

The mother of the two Boston bombing suspects, Zubeidat Tsarnaeva, speaks at a news conference in Makhachkala, the southern Russian province of Dagestan. At right is her sister-in-law Maryam, April 25, 2013. (AP Photo/Musa Sadulayev)

Tamerlan traveled to Russia last year and returned to the U.S. six months later, government officials told The Associated Press. More wasn't known about his travels.

According to law enforcement records he was arrested, in 2009, for assault and battery on a girlfriend; the charges were dismissed. His father told The New York Times that the case thwarted Tamerlan's hopes for U.S. citizenship.

Meanwhile, the mother of the suspects, Zubeidat Tsarnaev, was heard from only in an audio interview broadcast on CNN, defending her sons and calling the accusations against them a setup. She said she had never heard a word from her older son about any thinking that would have led to such an attack. "He never told me he would be on the side of jihad," she said.

Her younger son was described by friends as well-adjusted and well-liked in both high school and college, though at some point in college, his academic work reportedly suffered greatly.

"I'm in complete shock," said Rose Schutzberg, 19, who graduated high school with Dzhokhar and now attends Barnard College in New York. "He was a very studious person. He was really popular. He wrestled. People loved him."

In fact, Schutzberg said, she had "a little crush" on him in high school. "He's a great guy," she said. "He's smart, funny. He's definitely a really sweet person, very kind hearted, kind soul."

Dzhokhar was on the school's wrestling team. And in May 2011, his senior year, he was awarded a $2,500 scholarship from the city to pursue higher education, according to a news release at the time. That scholarship was celebrated with a reception at city hall.

The New Bedford Standard-Times reported that Dr. Brian Glyn Williams, who teaches Chechen history at the University of Massachusetts at Dartmouth, said he had tutored Dzhokhar in the subject when he was in high school.

"He was learning his Chechen identity, identifying with the diaspora and identifying with his homeland," Williams said, adding that Dzhokhar "wanted to learn more about Chechnya, who the fighters were, who the commanders were."

Dzhokhar went on to attend UMass-Dartmouth, according to university officials. He lived on the third floor of the Pine Dale dormitory. Harry Danso, who lives on the same floor, told the AP he saw him in a dorm hallway this week.

"He was regular, he was calm," said Danso.

The school would not say what he was studying. The father of the suspects, Anzor Tsarnaev, told the AP his younger son was "a second-year medical student," though he graduated high school in 2011.

"My son is a true angel ...," he said by telephone from the Russian city of Makhachkala. "He is such an intelligent boy. We expected him to come on holidays here."

Still, The New York Times reported that a college transcript revealed that he was failing many of his college classes. In two semesters in 2012 and 2013, he got seven failing grades, including F's in Principles of Modern Chemistry, Intro American Politics, and Chemistry and the Environment.

Dzhokhar's page on the Russian social networking site Vkontakte says that before moving to the United States, he attended School No. 1 in Makhachkala, the capital of Dagestan, and he describes himself as speaking Chechen as well as English and Russian. His world view is described as "Islam" and he says his personal goal is "career and money."

Deana Beaulieu, 20, lives two blocks away from the suspects' home on Norfolk Street, went to high school with Dzhokhar and was friendly with his sister.

Aliana Tsarnaeva, sister of Boston Marathon bombing suspect Dzhokhar Tsarnaev, departs district court in Boston's South Boston neighborhood, October 16, 2013. (AP Photo/Steven Senne)

Beaulieu says she doesn't recall Dzhokhar expressing any political views. "I thought he was going to branch off to college, and now this is what he's done. ... I don't understand what the hell happened, what set him off like this."

Florida Addy, 19, of Lynn, Mass., said she lived in the same college dorm with Dzhokhar this year and was on the same floor last year. She called him "drug" (pronounced droog), the Russian word for friend, a word he taught her.

Addy said she saw Dzhokhar last week, when she bummed a cigarette from him. They would occasionally hang out in his room or at the New Bedford apartment of Russian students he knew. He generally wore a hoodie or a white t-shirt and sweatpants, and spent a lot of his time with other kids from Russia.

She described him as down to earth and friendly, even a little mysterious, but in a charming way. She had just learned that he had a girlfriend, although she did not attend the university.

"He was nice. He was cool. I'm just in shock," she said.

Tim Kelleher, a wrestling coach for a Boston school that competed in 2010 against Dzhokhar's team, said the young man was a good wrestler, and that he'd never heard him express any political opinions.

"He was a tough, solid kid, just quiet," said Kelleher, now a Boston public school teacher.

Dzhokhar's uncle, too, was surprised by his suspected involvement in the attack much more, he said, than by his brother's. "It's not a surprise about him," Ruslan Tsarni, who lives in Maryland, said of Tamerlan. "The younger one, that's something else." He said the family had placed all its hopes with Dzhokhar, hoping he would be a doctor.

Tamerlan was more defined by sports, namely boxing. USA Boxing spokeswoman Julie Goldsticker said Tamerlan registered with the group as an amateur boxer from 2003 to 2004, and again from 2008 to 2010. He competed as a heavyweight in the National Golden Gloves competition in Salt Lake City on May 4, 2009, losing his only bout.

In photographs that appeared in the student magazine, including one in which he posed with his shirt off, Tamerlan has the muscular arms of a boxer, and is dressed in flashy street-clothes that he said were "European style."

In another window onto his personality, his Amazon wish list traced by the AP using an email address on his public record report includes books on organized crime, document forgery, the conflict in Chechnya, and two self-help books, including Dale Carnegie's "How to Win Friends & Influence People."

Gene McCarthy, who trained Tamerlan at the Somerville Boxing Club, described him as a "nice kid" who already was a good fighter before he showed up at the gym years ago.

"He never lost a bout for me," McCarthy said. "He had some skills from his father before he showed up in my gym." McCarthy described the young man as "very intelligent" and recalled that he also played classical piano.

In Kyrgyzstan, the former Soviet republic where the family lived before it moved to Dagestan, Leila Alieva, a former schoolmate, remembers an educated family and a nice boy.

"He was ... a good student, a jock, a boxer. He used to win all the (boxing) competitions in town," she said. "I can't believe they were involved in the explosions, because Tamerlan was a very positive guy, and they were not very Islamist. They were Muslim, but had a secular lifestyle."

The Al-Barzakh Islamic Cemetery where Boston bombing suspect Tamerlan Tsarnaev is buried in Doswell, Va., May 13, 2013. (AP Photo/Cliff Owen)

In a local news article in 2004, Tamerlan spoke about his boxing and his views of America.

"I like the USA," Tamerlan was quoted as saying in The Sun of Lowell, Mass. "America has a lot of jobs. That's something Russia doesn't have. You have a chance to make money here if you are willing to work."

BOSTON SUSPECTS' CHECHEN FAMILY TRAVELED LONG ROAD
April 20, 2013
By Leila Saralayeva

The two brothers accused of blowing up homemade bombs at the Boston Marathon came from a Chechen family that for decades had been tossed from one country to another by war and persecution.

Their father and former neighbors from Kyrgyzstan, home to many Chechens who were deported from their native villages by Soviet dictator Josef Stalin, tell of a family often on the move in search of safety and a better life.

Tamerlan Tsarnaev, 26, who was killed in a shootout, and his 19-year-old brother, Dzhokhar Tsarnaev, who was captured alive, had moved to the United States about a decade ago with their parents and two sisters. By all accounts, the younger brother had many friends, but his older brother felt alienated from American society and in recent years had turned increasingly to Islam.

Although neither spent much time in Chechnya, a province in southern Russia that has been torn apart by war and an Islamic insurgency, both strongly identified themselves as Chechens. They took up boxing and wrestling, two of the most popular sports in Chechnya, where people are proud of their warrior traditions.

The brothers' story begins in Tokmok, a town about 60 kilometers (35 miles) from the capital of Kyrgyzstan, a country in Central Asia that was once part of the Soviet Union. Stalin rounded up the Chechens and shipped them east during World War II, seeing them as potentially disloyal. Their father, Anzor Tsarnaev, was born in Kyrgyzstan.

"This was a very good family," Badrudi Tsokoev, a fellow Chechen who lived next door to the Tsarnaevs, said Saturday. "They all strove to get a higher education, to somehow set themselves up in life."

The brothers' grandfather had died tragically when a shell exploded as he was scavenging for metal that could be sold as scrap, neighbors said.

After the 1991 collapse of the Soviet Union, the family moved to Chechnya, only to have war break out in 1994 between Russian troops and Chechen separatists fighting for an independent homeland. Dzhokhar was born in 1993 and shares the name of Chechnya's first separatist leader.

The fierce battles, which reduced much of Chechnya to rubble, sent the Tsarnaevs fleeing back to Kyrgyzstan with their two young sons, a daughter and another one on the way.

"As soon as the war started they came back," said Nadezhda Nazarenko, another former neighbor in Tokmok. The children's mother "described how they were in clothes they would wear only around the house and fled the bombing, managing only to grab their documents and a few things."

Neighbors said Anzor Tsarnaev, who had studied law and previously served in the prosecutor's office, worked hard to provide for his family.

Zubeidat Tsarnaeva, the mother of the two Boston bombing suspects, speaks at a news conference as the suspects' father, Anzor Tsarnaev listens in Makhachkala, in the southern Russian province of Dagestan, April 25, 2013. (AP Photo/Musa Sadulayev)

"Soon they began to live well and renovated their home," Nazarenko said. "The children did well in school and were well behaved."

Russian troops rolled into Chechnya again in 1999 and took it under Moscow's control. The same year, the Tsarnaev family moved back to Russia, according to Anzor Tsarnaev, settling briefly in Dagestan, which like neighboring Chechnya is a predominantly Muslim republic. They left from there in 2002 for the United States, joining relatives who had emigrated earlier.

Anzor Tsarnaev told The Associated Press that the move to the U.S. was motivated in part by a desire to escape discrimination against Chechens in Russia and Kyrgyzstan.

He returned about a year ago to Dagestan, which has become the epicenter of the Islamic insurgency that spilled over from Chechnya to spread throughout the North Caucasus region.

His elder son visited him last year, according to neighbors in Makhachkala, the capital of Dagestan.

No evidence has emerged to connect Tamerlan Tsarnaev with the insurgents, who have carried out a series of terrorist attacks in Russia. The FBI said it interviewed him in 2011 at the request of an unspecified foreign government and found nothing of concern at the time.

Anzor Tsarnaev visited his hometown in Kyrgyzstan last year, according to Tsokoev, the former neighbor. "He was very happy and proud of his sons' success in the U.S.," Tsokoev said. "We also were happy for him. He worked hard to give his children a good education."

Tsarnaev, who worked as an auto mechanic in the U.S., seems unable to comprehend that his sons could have been involved in such a gruesome bombing.

"These children were brought up with kindness," Tsarnaev said in an interview shown Saturday on Russian television. "We're a family of lawyers, and everyone who knows us knows that."

FOR BOMBING SUSPECTS, QUESTION MAY BE WHO LED WHOM
April 21, 2013
By Allen G. Breed, Eric Tucker and Jeff Donn

Tamerlan Tsarnaev ranted at a neighbor about Islam and the United States. His younger brother, Dzhokhar, relished debating people on religion, "then crushing their beliefs with facts."

The older brother sought individual glory in the boxing ring, while the younger excelled as part of a team. Tamerlan "swaggered" through the family home like a "man-of-the-house type," one visitor recalls, while Dzhokhar seemed "very respectful and very obedient" to his mother.

The brothers, now forever linked in the Boston Marathon bombing tragedy, in some ways seemed as different as siblings could be. But whatever drove them to allegedly set off two pressure-cooker bombs, their uncle is certain Dzhokhar was not the one pulling the strings.

Zubeidat Tsarnaeva, left, and husband Anzor Tsarnaev show videos on an iPad they say show their sons could not have been involved in last month's Boston Marathon bombings in their new apartment in Makhachkala, regional capital of Dagestan, Russia, May 30, 2013. (AP Photo/Musa Sadulayev)

"He's not been understanding anything. He's a 19-year-old boy," Ruslan Tsarni said of his brother's youngest child, who is clinging to life in a Boston hospital after a gun battle with police.

"He's been absolutely wasted by his older brother. I mean, he used him. He used him for whatever he's done. For what we see they've done. OK?"

Criminologist James Alan Fox says the uncle's intuition is justified. In cases like this, he says, it is highly unusual for the younger participant in this case, a sibling to be the leader.

"I would be surprised," says Fox, a professor of Criminology, Law and Public Policy at Boston's Northeastern University. "Very surprised."

Whatever their fraternal pecking order, when the bullets began flying in Watertown on Thursday night and 26-year-old Tamerlan went down, his younger brother ran him over dragging him for about 30 feet before ditching the car and fleeing on foot. After a 24-hour manhunt that shut down most of the Boston metropolitan area, police cornered the gravely wounded Dzhokhar hiding in a boat in a backyard, only blocks from where his brother bled out.

Officials said Dzhokhar was in serious condition Saturday, unable to communicate. So, at least for now, investigators and the public are left with only enigma.

The ethnic Chechen family came to this country in 2002, after fleeing troubles in Kyrgyzstan and then Dagestan, a predominantly Muslim republic in Russia's North Caucasus. They settled in a working-class part of Cambridge, where the father, Anzor Tsarnaev, opened an auto shop.

He returned to Dagestan about a year ago.

Luis Vasquez went to high school with Tamerlan and later helped coach Dzhokhar's soccer team at Cambridge Rindge and Latin. With the father gone, Vasquez said, the older brother assumed a kind of paternal role, at least where the girls in the family were concerned.

"He was very protective of his (younger) sister, Bella," Vasquez said. "He would keep an eye out, making sure she's good, making sure she's not having a hard time."

Vasquez chalked it up to "his culture" and "what his family expected out of him."

David Mijares, who trained in boxing with Tamerlan in high school and later coached the younger brother in soccer, agreed that his friend felt pressure to take his father's place.

"He had to be a man at a very early age," says Mijares. "That would be, in my opinion, a huge reason for who he was, all serious and no nonsense."

John Pinto said the pair were frequent patrons at his Midwest Grill, just a couple of blocks from their house. When they walked in, he said, Tamerlan was always in the lead.

"I think the big brother is more the command guy, boss," Pinto said, puffing out his chest for emphasis.

That said, Dzhokhar was very much his own man. While he would tag along to Tamerlan's boxing practices, the younger brother was into wrestling.

In one of his tweets, he complained that his mother was trying to arrange a marriage for him, as she'd done for his sisters.

"she needs to (hash) chillout," he tweeted on July 12. "i'll find my own honey."

Tamerlan preceded his brother at the prestigious Cambridge Rindge and Latin High School, which counts celebrities Matt Damon and Ben Affleck among its alumni. But he does not appear to have been a standout student and athlete whose reputation Dzhokhar would have felt pressure to live up to.

"To be perfectly honest, I did not know he HAD an older brother from the start," said classmate Alexandros Stefanakis, who played pickup basketball games and hung out with Dzhokhar outside school.

Anne Kilzer of Belmont would go to the Tsarnaev home for regular facials from the boys' mother, Zubeidat. She said the older brother was a "macho guy," whereas Dzhokhar seemed more cerebral.

The few times that Tamerlan was there, he would wave his mother off when she tried to introduce him. "He sort of swaggered through," she said. "Sort of a man-of-the-house type."

In a blog entry, Kilzer's daughter, Alyssa, suggested that the mother became increasingly religious as their acquaintance progressed. For instance, she began wearing a hijab, the traditional Muslim headscarf.

"She started to refuse to see boys that had gone through puberty, as she had consulted a religious figure and he had told her it was sacrilegious," Alyssa Kilzer wrote. "She was often fasting. She told me that she had cried for days when her oldest son, Tamerlan, told her that he wanted to move out, going against her culture's tradition of the son staying in the house with the mother until marriage."

She said the mother also expressed some rather strident views about the U.S. government. But it was difficult to know who was influencing whom in the household.

"During this facial session she started quoting a conspiracy theory, telling me that she thought 9-11 was purposefully created by the American government to make America hate Muslims," Alyssa Kilzer wrote. "`It's real,' she said. `My son knows all about it. You can read on the internet.'"

Kilzer didn't say to which son the mother was referring. Kilzer, who is studying in Scotland, could not immediately be reached.

Tsarni told The Associated Press from his home in Maryland that a deep rift opened between him and his sister-in-law, but that he tried to maintain a relationship with the boys. However, that effort began to fall apart several years ago, he said, when Tamerlan "started carrying all this nonsense associated with religion, with Islamic religion."

When he asked his older nephew why he wasn't in school, he said Tamerlan gave an enigmatic answer. "Oh, I'm in God's business," the young man replied.

Ruslan Tsarni, the uncle of the Boston Marathon bombing suspect, speaks with the media outside his home in Montgomery Village in Md. In the years before the Boston Marathon bombings, Tamerlan Tsarnaev fell under the influence of a new friend, a Muslim convert who steered the religiously apathetic young man toward a strict strain of Islam, family members said. "Somehow, he just took his brain," said Tsarni, who recalled conversations with Tamerlan's worried father about the friend of Tamerlan's known only to the family as Misha, April 19, 2013. (AP Photo/Jose Luis Magana, File)

Tamerlan would throw out foreign words like "jihad" and "Inshallah" Arabic for "God willing" without really understanding their meaning, he said. Though Tsarni is himself Muslim, he said he does not worship at a mosque.

Katherine Russell, right, wife of Boston Marathon bomber suspect Tamerlan Tsarnaev, leaves the law office of DeLuca and Weizenbaum Monday, April 29, 2013, in Providence, R.I. (AP Photo/Stew Milne)

The uncle was surprised when he learned that Tamerlan had gotten married to an American woman a "good Christian family girl," who his nephew said was about to convert to Islam.

In February, Alexander Podobryaev, who lives a couple of houses from the Tsarnaevs, exchanged pleasantries with Tamerlan as they shoveled snow. He says the man pointed to a woman in a black Muslim headscarf and identified her as his wife.

Others began noticing signs of Tamerlan's increasing agitation.

One of the brothers' neighbors, Albrecht Ammon, said he had a bizarre encounter with Tamerlan in a pizza shop about three months ago. The older brother argued with him about U.S. foreign policy, the wars in Afghanistan and Iraq, and religion.

He said Tamerlan referred to the Bible as a "cheap copy" of the Quran, and that many of this country's wars "are based upon the Bible how it's an excuse to invade other countries."

"He had nothing against the American people," Ammon said. "He had something against the American government."

Dzhokhar, on the other hand, was "real cool," Ammon said. "A chill guy."

An elder at the Islamic Society of Boston Cultural Center, the largest mosque in New England, said Tamerlan occasionally attended Friday prayer services at the mosque in the past year and a half.

About three months ago, around Martin Luther King Day, Tamerlan stood up and interrupted the imam during the sermon, said Anwar Kazmi, a board member of the Islamic Society. The imam compared the slain civil rights leads to the Prophet Muhammed, drawing objections from Tamerlan, Kazmi said.

Mosque leaders later sat down with Tamerlan and discussed his rant, said Kazmi, who said Tamerlan returned to future services and had no further outbursts.

While his older brother was railing about religion and world politics, Dzhokhar seemed more interested in the HBO series "Game of Thrones" and other television shows.

"Breaking Bad taught me how to dispose of a corpse," he tweeted on Jan. 16, referring to the popular AMC series about a dying chemistry teacher who turns to cooking methamphetamine to leave a nest egg for his family.

He did tweet about religion, but they were hardly the words of a hard-core zealot.

"This night deserves Hennessy a bad b---- and an o of weed," he wrote on Nov. 17. "the holy trinity"

On Nov. 29, he wrote: "I kind of like religious debates, just hearing what other people believe is interesting and then crushing their beliefs with facts is fun." And on Jan. 15: "I don't argue with fools who say Islam is terrorism it's not worth a thing, let an idiot remain an idiot."

However, he acknowledged in another message around Christmas that the "Brothers at the mosque either think I'm a convert or that I'm from Algeria or Syria."

Fox said it's not unheard of for the younger person in a crime team to be the dominant personality. But he said it's rare.

"In this case, the older brother is the one that seems to have become religious and drawn to Islam," Fox said. "The older brother dropped out of school ... whereas the younger brother, it was all positives."

Tamerlan was a fairly gifted boxer, but he preened about fighting prowess that often fell far short. His younger brother seemed content to be part of a team.

Marvin Salazar was two years older than Dzhokhar when they attended Community Charter Schools of Cambridge, where they played intramural soccer together. He was impressed by the younger boy's smarts and drive, but noted that while Dzhokhar was very fast, he wasn't the kind of kid who needed to showboat and score goals.

"I remember he told me he liked to play midfield," the 21-year-old said. "He's the guy who sets everybody up for the plays. He's one of the most important people."

He was also on his high school wrestling team.

Tamerlan once said he had no American friends. His brother had lots of them, but fellow students at UMass-Dartmouth say he also hung out with some Russian speakers.

On March 14, 2012, Dzhokhar tweeted: "a decade in america already, i want out" That same day, he added, "im trying to grow a beard."

Dzhokhar became naturalized last September, federal officials told the AP. His older brother had a green card but may have been thwarted in his quest for U.S. citizenship by an assault charge, his father told The New York Times.

If Tamerlan recorded his thoughts, they have not yet surfaced at least publicly. His brother left a trail on the Internet, although in an Aug. 7, 2012 tweet, he called himself a "heavy sleeper and a great liar."

In March, Dzhokhar tweeted: "Evil triumphs when good men do nothing." A week and a half earlier, he reminded his followers, "Never underestimate the rebel with a cause."

The day of the bombing, he wrote: "There are people that know the truth but stay silent & there are people that speak the truth but we don't hear them cuz they're the minority"

Tsarni is confident authorities will find that Tamerlan was his "Dzhokhar, of course, was looking up at him," he said.

But their body language the day of the bombings seems to suggest at least a partnership of equals.

In one of the now infamous photos the FBI released to the public in hopes of tips, the older brother has his head down, the visor pulled low over his face as if he's trying to hide. Dzhokhar, by contrast, has his white baseball cap turned backward, revealing his entire face, his chin is thrust confidently into the air.

FBI INTERVIEWED TAMERLAN TSARNAEV AFTER 2011 TIP
April 20, 2013
By Pete Yost

The Russian FSB intelligence security service told the FBI in early 2011 about information that Tamerlan Tsarnaev, one of the brothers suspected in the Boston Marathon bombings, was a follower of radical Islam, two law enforcement officials said Saturday.

Tamerlan Tsarnaev died in a shootout, and his younger brother was captured alive. They were identified by authorities and relatives as ethnic Chechens from southern Russia who had been in the U.S. for about a decade.

According to an FBI news release issued Friday night (April 19), a foreign government said that based on its information, Tsarnaev was a strong believer and that he had changed drastically since 2010 as he prepared to leave the U.S. for travel to the Russian region to join unspecified underground groups.

The FBI did not name the foreign government, but the two law enforcement officials identified the FSB as the provider of the information to one of the FBI's field offices and also to FBI headquarters in Washington. The two officials spoke on condition of anonymity because they were not authorized to speak on the record about the matter.

The FBI said that in response, it interviewed Tsarnaev and relatives, and did not find any domestic or foreign terrorism activity. The FBI said it provided the results in the summer of 2011. The FBI also said that it requested but did not receive more specific or additional information from the foreign government.

The bureau added that in response to the request, it checked U.S. government databases and other information to look for such things as derogatory telephone communications, possible use of online sites associated with the promotion of radical activity, associations with other persons of interest, travel history and plans and education history.

5

VICTIMS

Boston Police Commissioner Edward Davis testifies before the House Homeland Security Committee at a hearing on "The Boston Bombings: A First Look," on Capitol Hill in Washington. Photos of those who were killed at the Boston Marathon bombing are at right, May 9, 2013. (AP Photo/Susan Walsh)

MARATHON VICTIMS HAD NAILS, PELLETS IN WOUNDS
April 16, 2013
By Marilynn Marchione

A dark-haired little girl arrived with singed eyebrows, nails sticking out of her and a badly damaged leg. A little boy also was full of metal fragments, one of his legs bound by a tourniquet that saved his life. A day later, the injuries from the Boston Marathon explosions are now more of a threat to limbs than to lives, doctors and hospitals report.

Three people were killed and more than 170 people were injured by two bombs that were reportedly packed with pellets, nails or metal shards. Dozens remain hospitalized with broken bones, shredded muscles and head injuries. At least a dozen people lost one or more limbs from blasts that doctors say are typical of war zones and leave combat-style injuries. And some described horrific scenes, such as seeing a severed foot on the pavement.

Investigators found fragments of BBs and nails, possibly contained in a pressure cooker used to make the explosives. Doctors' accounts reflected that description.

"We've removed BBs and we've removed nails from kids. One of the sickest things for me was just to see nails sticking out of a little girl's body," said Dr. David Mooney, trauma chief at Boston Children's Hospital, which treated 10 blast victims, including a pregnant woman later transferred to another medical center.

Mooney at first doubted the emergency call to prepare for many seriously injured patients. Then he saw the 10-year-old boy with the badly injured leg.

"My first thought was, `He's really hurt. This isn't just some EMS overcall,'" Mooney said. "Someone at the scene put on a big tourniquet. He had singed hair, singed eyebrows, soot all over his face."

The 9-year-old girl also was in bad shape and singed. "Whoever got to her first saved her life" by putting on a tourniquet, Mooney said. "If they hadn't done that, she would have died."

Fast work by emergency responders no doubt saved many lives, doctors at many Boston area hospitals said. The blast occurred near the marathon's finish line where medical tents were set up to care for injured or tired runners.

People at the scene used different things as tourniquets, including lanyards with marathon credentials many wore around their necks. Some police officers gave their belts, said Dr. Martin Levine, a New Jersey family physician who was one of the doctors being paid to help elite athletes recover after they finish the race.

Levine told of a woman whose right leg was severed at her right thigh, leaving the femur bone sticking out, and of seeing a severed foot on the ground and not knowing whose it was.

"I've never seen an explosion where people's bodies explode and I hope I never see it again," he said.

When word of mass casualties reached Tufts Medical Center, "we stopped all elective surgery in the operating room" in order to free up rooms to treat blast victims, said Dr. William Mackey, the hospitals' surgery chief.

Doctors removed many odd-shaped pieces of metal ranging up to half an inch in size, with nurses saving and tagging them for waiting police investigators.

"One woman from the blast had a piece of a zipper, a handle of a zipper embedded in her ankle joint, which is indicative of the force of the explosion," he said. Of the 19 blast patients, 10 remained at the hospital as of midday Tuesday (April 16).

Dr. Brien Barnewolt, chair of emergency medicine at Tufts Medical Center in Boston, speaks to reporters at the hospital, Tuesday, April 16, 2013. (AP Photo/Josh Reynolds)

At Beth Israel Deaconess Medical Center, Dr. Stephen Epstein said he saw an X-ray of one victim's leg that had "what appears to be small, uniform, round objects throughout it similar in the appearance to BBs."

The hospital treated 24 patients, including three amputations. As of Tuesday morning nine patients had been sent home.

Doctors at Massachusetts General Hospital treated 31 victims. The hospital performed four amputations and at least two more patients have legs that are still at risk of amputation, Dr. George Velmahos said.

At Boston Medical Center, the trauma chief, Dr. Peter Burke, said 19 of the 23 blast victims it treated remain hospitalized, 10 in critical condition. Five patients have lost one or more limbs.

"Some of those 10 are pretty sick" and may yet wind up needing amputations, he said. A lot of them are kept on life-support for multiple operations, but the staff expects and hopes all will survive, he said.

An orthopedic trauma surgeon there, Dr. Paul Tornetta, described pellets and metal shards in many wounds.

"This is very high energy, high velocity shrapnel and blast injuries ... very similar to what a hand grenade might do," he said.

Many of the injuries sound similar to those caused by IED attacks in Iraq and Afghanistan, said Dr. Andrew Pollak, chair of an American Academy of Orthopedic Surgeons' war injuries project. Pollak, an orthopedic trauma surgeon at the University of Maryland, said he's heard about the injuries from colleagues in Boston. Improvised explosive devices are often packed with nails, ball bearings and sharp pieces of metal designed to inflict severe injuries. Blast victims face a huge risk of infection because of debris that gets imbedded in tissue, Pollak said.

STORIES OF THE DEAD AND INJURED
April 18, 2013
By The Associated Press

The twin bombs at the Boston Marathon killed three people and wounded more than 170 on Monday. Here are the stories of those killed and some of the injured.

LU LINGZI: A LONG WAY FROM HOME
She was a food fan, eager for culinary discoveries. In her last blog update the morning before the Boston Marathon blasts, the Chinese graduate student identified as the attack's third victim posted a photo of bread chunks and fruit.

"My wonderful breakfast," Boston University statistics student Lu Lingzi wrote.

Lingzi, in her early 20s, often shared photos of her home-prepared meals online a blueberry-covered waffle one day, spinach sacchettini with zucchini on another. In September, she showed off her first two-dish meal stir-fried broccoli and scrambled eggs with tomatoes, often cooked by Chinese students learning how to live on their own abroad.

Tasso Kaper, the chair of BU's mathematics department, says Lu loved flowers and the springtime. She had only one course left in order to graduate.

She was standing with two friends when the bombs went off. One was seriously injured.

The Boston Red Sox stand during tribute to Boston Marathon bombing victims, including Chinese student Lu Lingzi, before a baseball game against the Kansas City Royals in Boston, April 20, 2013. (AP Photo/Michael Dwyer)

THE RICHARDS: A FAMILY INJURED, IN MOURNING

Neighbors and friends remembered 8-year-old bombing victim Martin Richard as a vivacious boy who loved to run, climb and play sports like soccer, basketball and baseball.

The boy's father, Bill Richard, released a statement thanking family, friends and strangers for their support following his son's death Monday. Richard's wife, Denise, and the couple's 6-year-old daughter, Jane, also suffered significant injuries in the blasts.

The family was watching Monday's race and had gone to get ice cream before returning to the area near the finish line before the blasts.

Denise Richard works as a librarian at the Neighborhood House Charter School, where Martin was a third-grader and Jane attends first grade. Counselors were being made available to staff and students.

"I just can't get a handle on it," family friend Jack Cunningham said of the boy's death. "In an instant, life changes."

KRYSTLE CAMPBELL: CHEERING ON FRIENDS

Krystle Campbell was a 29-year-old restaurant manager from Medford. Her father, 56-year-old William Campbell, described her as "just a very caring, very loving person, and was daddy's little girl."

Campbell had gone to the race with her best friend Karen, whose boyfriend was running in the race, her father said.

A photo of Krystle Campbell, 29, hangs at a makeshift memorial near the finish line of Boston Marathon explosions, April 18, 2013. (AP Photo/Matt Rourke)

"They wanted to take a photograph of him crossing the finish line, but the explosion went off and they were right there," he said. "It's pretty devastating."

The friend suffered a severe leg injury.

Krystle's grandmother told multiple media outlets that the family was initially told Campbell was alive because of a name mix-up. When her father arrived at Massachusetts General Hospital, however, he learned that his daughter had died.

Krystle's grandmother, Lillian Campbell, said somewhere on the way to the hospital, their names got mixed up.

Lillian Campbell said her son was "devastated" when he found out the truth and almost passed out.

PATRICK AND JESSICA DOWNES: NEWLYWEDS

Patrick and Jessica Downes married in August. According to an email sent to friends, Patrick had surgery Wednesday and is out of intensive care, while Jessica was in surgery. Both lost their left leg below the knee, and Jessica was in danger of losing her remaining foot.

Friends who set up a page at GiveForward.com to raise money for the couple's expenses said they first started dating in 2006.

Patrick graduated from Boston College and was so well-behaved in high school that he was nicknamed "Jesus." They described him as the "ultimate Boston boy."

"He has that accent that makes it impossible to tell if he's saying `parking' or `packing,' he's no more than two degrees of separation from Whitey Bulger (or so he claims), and he cried his eyes out when the Sox finally won the World Series," the site said.

Jessica, described as a sassy California girl, is a nurse at Massachusetts General Hospital.

"She has the spirit of a lion," the site said.

A spokesman for GiveForward.com said the page got so many hits Wednesday that it crashed.

AARON HERN: A TOUGH COOKIE

Eleven-year-old Aaron Hern was there with his father, Alan, and little sister, Abby, to cheer on his mother, Katherine, in her first Boston Marathon when the bomb went off. After initially becoming separated, Alan found his son lying injured on the ground with leg wounds.

"He was conscious, he talked to me and said, `My leg really hurts, daddy,' but he was being pretty brave," Alan Hern told KGO-TV.

The family is from Martinez, Calif., and Alan Hern is the Alhambra High School varsity football coach, KGO reported.

Aaron remained in critical condition at Boston Children's Hospital on Wednesday and underwent three to four hours of surgery on his leg, the hospital said.

His mother said in a note posted online by Kiwanis Club of Martinez that Aaron was trying harder and harder to communicate through a touchpad. She said it was stressful because he was starting to remember everything and getting upset.

The mother of Aaron's best friend, Katherine Chapman, told The San Francisco Chronicle that Aaron was an outgoing and fun-loving kid.

"A tough cookie, an athlete and a scholar. He gets good grades and participates in every sport and is good at everything he does. He's one of those kids that everybody loves," she said.

His 12th birthday is May 1.

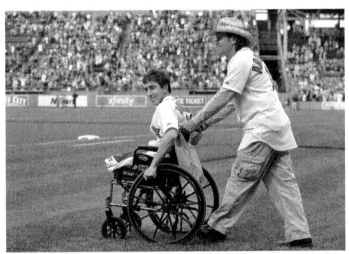

Boston Marathon bombing survivor Jeff Bauman, left, is wheeled out by Carlos Arredondo, the man who helped save his life, to throw out the ceremonial first pitch at Fenway Park prior to a baseball game between the Boston Red Sox and the Philadelphia Phillies, in Boston. Bauman is working on a memoir with Grand Central Publishing to be titled "Stronger," scheduled to come out in April, May 28, 2013. (AP Photo/Elise Amendola)

JEFF BAUMAN JR.: LOST BOTH LEGS

Jeff Bauman Jr., a man pictured in an Associated Press photo from immediately after the blast, lost both his legs as cheered his girlfriend on in the race. He survived the trauma after people rushed him away from the explosion site in a wheelchair.

Rescuers took the 27-year-old victim to Boston Medical Center, but doctors had to amputate his legs because of extensive vascular and bone damage, a Facebook post from his father said Tuesday.

"Unfortunately my son was just in the wrong place at the wrong time," the elder Jeff Bauman wrote.

The son also had to have more surgery later because of fluid in his abdomen. His condition improved later.

"I just can't explain what's wrong with people today to do this to people," the father wrote. "I'm really starting to lose faith in our country."

BRITTANY LORING: AN AMBITIOUS STUDENT

Brittany Loring was spending Monday, her 29th birthday, cheering on her friend in the Boston Marathon. A day later, she lay in critical condition with injuries to her head, leg and fingers.

Heather Abbott, center, who lost part of her left leg in the 2013 Boston Marathon explosion, is assisted by physical therapist Dan Connors, top right, as she performs an agility drill during a running clinic for challenged athletes, October 6, 2013. (AP Photo/Steven Senne)

"We've had so many calls. Everybody's just upset over it," grandmother Philomena Loring told the Lowell Sun. "I put her on the prayer line at my church."

Loring is simultaneously pursuing degrees in law and business administration at Boston College. She's also a runner, finishing 80th in the Boston College MBA 5K on April 6.

HEATHER ABBOTT: BEST FRIEND TURNED, FOUND HER GONE

Heather Abbott, of Newport, R.I., was entering a bar with friends as the bomb went off. Her best friend, Jason Geremia, told WJAR-TV that everyone ran out the back. Once he got there, he realized Abbott wasn't with him. He turned to go back when he saw a bouncer carrying her down the stairs.

"I said, `Give her to me. Give her to me.' And he was like, `Do you know her?' I said, `Yes, yes. That's my best friend.' I said, `Give her to me.' He said, `No, no, no. Look at her leg.' It was very tough to see that."

Her leg was severely injured. Another friend took off his belt, and they used it as a tourniquet.

Geremia spent much of Monday and Tuesday at the hospital, along with Abbott's parents, who are from Lincoln, R.I.

"It's very, very hard to see her," Geremia said.

JARROD CLOWERY: `GET INTO THE STREET'

Jarrod Clowery and his friends were cheering on spectators when he heard the first explosion.

"I got this feeling that we need to get into the street," Clowery said.

Clowery, 35, a carpenter, hopped over one of the metal barricades that separates spectators on the sidewalk from runners on the course when the second blast went off behind him.

"Because I was elevated on the railing I think I avoided major, major injury," Clowery said, adding that his friends were injured much more severely.

Clowery said his hearing was diminished by about 85 percent. He has shrapnel embedded in the back of his leg and suffered flash burns.

"The Lord was watching over me, somebody was watching over me," Clowery said. "And I feel very blessed."

JOHN ODOM: CHEERING HIS DAUGHTER

John Odom's daughter, Nicole Reis, was running the marathon as a member of the New England Patriots Charitable Foundation Marathon team, and he was there to support her. Her husband, Matt Reis, is the goalie for the Major League Soccer team the New England Revolution.

Odom was around 10 feet away from the first bomb when it went off, Matt Reis told reporters at Gillette Stadium in Foxborough on Wednesday, where he visited to thank teammates for their support. Odom remained in critical condition and had undergone three surgeries in about 40 hours, he said.

"He hasn't really stabilized yet, and we're still hoping," he said. "He is progressing a little bit, but we're talking about footsteps here and not very big strides."

**BOSTON BOMB SURVIVOR, 7,
USING NEW PROSTHETIC LEG**
August 16, 2013
By The Associated Press

The family of 2013 Boston Marathon bombing victim Martin Richard, from left, mother Denise, brother Henry, and father Bill Richard, place their hands over their hearts as they stand with former Boston Mayor Tom Menino, right, during a tribute in honor of the one year anniversary of the Boston Marathon bombings in Boston. At left is a Mass. State Trooper, April 15, 2014. (AP Photo/Charles Krupa)

A 7-year-old girl who lost part of her left leg in the Boston Marathon bombings is learning to use a prosthetic leg as her family still mourns the death of her older brother in the April attack.

The family of Jane Richard and the late 8-year-old Martin Richard said Thursday (August 15) she already is dancing on her prosthetic leg and "struts around on it with great pride."

"While we have made progress with our physical injuries, the emotional pain seems every bit as new as it was four months ago," the Richard family said in a statement Thursday.

Parents Bill and Denise Richard also were hurt in the attack April 15, when two shrapnel-loaded pressure cookers exploded near the marathon's finish line, killing three people and injuring about 260 others. Denise Richard lost sight in one eye, and Bill Richard suffered hearing loss. Their 11-year-old son, Henry Richard, was uninjured.

Authorities say two ethnic Chechen brothers from Russia living in the Boston area orchestrated the attack. Dzhokhar Tsarnaev, 20, has pleaded not guilty. His older brother Tamerlan Tsarnaev, 26, died following a gun battle with police three days after the bombings.

The Richards say they're still coping with the agony of losing Martin "and the senseless way it came about."

"The pain is constant, and even the sweetest moments can become heartbreaking when we are struck by the realization that, `Martin would have loved this,'" they said in their statement.

Jane came home from a rehab hospital a few weeks ago. That night, the family slept together at their home in the city's Dorchester neighborhood for the first time since Martin's death. They'd been determined none of them would sleep in their own beds "until all of us could do so."

The Richards said Henry and Jane return to school in a few weeks and the family will begin exploring a "meaningful and impactful way" to honor Martin's memory.

VICTIM IN FAMOUS PHOTO MARKS YEAR SINCE MARATHON
April 5, 2014
By Michelle R. Smith

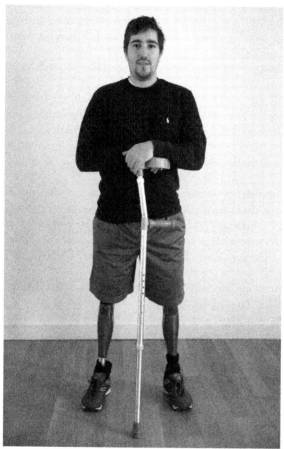

Jeff Bauman stands in his home in Carlisle, Mass., March 14, 2014. (AP Photo/Charles Krupa)

The year since Jeff Bauman was pushed in a wheelchair from the Boston Marathon, his legs ravaged and his face ashen, has been marked by pain and difficulty but also by triumphs: He's learned to walk on new prosthetic legs, he's gotten engaged and he's an expectant father.

Bauman became one of the most recognizable and powerful symbols of Boston's resilience after the April 15 attacks - immortalized in an Associated Press photo that shows three rescuers rushing him from the scene. He became a hero days later when he was able to help authorities identify one of two brothers accused of setting off pressure cooker bombs, killing two women and an 8-year-old boy and injuring more than 260 others. His memoir, "Stronger," comes out Tuesday.

The past year has been a blur for Bauman, and he can't get used to the idea that this is his new life.

"Right now, you know, it's kind of a challenge to put my legs on every day. I'm not used to it. It's something unnatural for me. But I think over time it will become more of a natural thing," Bauman, 28, told the AP in an interview at the home he shares with his fiancée, Erin Hurley. "At first I couldn't even wear them for 20 minutes. ... Now, I can wear them all day."

Bauman was standing near the finish line with two friends, waiting to cheer on Hurley as she completed the marathon, one of the most important and busiest events of the year in the city. He noticed a man who looked out of place in a crowd of revelers, and they exchanged a long stare. As Bauman describes him, he was "all business."

Moments later, the two bombs exploded. Bauman found himself on the ground, his legs gone. People rushed in to help, but Bauman thought it was the end. Suddenly, a man in a cowboy hat appeared: Carlos Arredondo. He lifted Bauman into a wheelchair pushed by Devin Wang, a Boston University student, and they rushed toward the medical tents. They were joined along the way by Paul Mitchell, an EMT with Boston EMS.

"When someone looks that way, they've lost a lot of blood, and they're really close to being dead," Mitchell said.

Thanks to his rescuers, he lived. He was in surgery within 20 minutes at Boston Medical Center.

Soon after Bauman woke, he was able to provide a description of the man who was "all business." Authorities say it was Tamerlan Tsarnaev, who was killed in a shootout with police in Watertown days later. Tsarnaev's brother, Dzhokhar, has pleaded not guilty and is awaiting trial.

Bauman calls the brothers "weak" and says they wasted their lives. He said Dzhokhar Tsarnaev must suffer from knowing what he did, especially killing a child.

"You can't tell me that that doesn't eat away at that kid every single day. It has to. It must haunt him," he said. "Or if it doesn't, it eventually will."

Bauman has focused on healing and learning to manage his new legs. He lost his legs above the knee, making it harder to adjust to his prosthetics. It takes more energy to walk with prosthetics than it does to walk normally, which means he gets tired easily.

He has made steady progress, and by March, he was walking with one crutch. He hopes to someday be able to walk without the crutches and to use the prosthetics all day without his legs getting sore, as they do now.

Sleeping was tough for him the first few months, and he still has nights when his mind is racing too fast to get any sleep. Days can be tough, too.

"I have bad days, days when I just don't want to do anything. Just kind of want to lay in bed," he said. "I don't want to see anybody today. There's days like that."

Bauman is on leave from the Costco store where he worked in Nashua, N.H., before the bombing. He wants to learn how to drive again before going back, and he has a rigorous rehabilitation schedule that requires several appointments a week. He also feels he's not prepared mentally to return yet.

For now, Bauman and Hurley are preparing for the baby, due July 14. They got engaged in February and tentatively plan to get married next year, Hurley said.

Bauman admits he has some jitters.

"I'm kind of scared, I don't know. I mean, I just want to be able to be there physically when the baby's running around and going nuts," he said.

They don't know yet if it's a boy or a girl. To be safe, Bauman painted the nursery a neutral shade of gray. The couple moved into a home in rural Carlisle, northwest of Boston, in the fall. Before then, Bauman lived with his mother in an apartment in Chelmsford, an old mill town to the north.

Hurley says Bauman is still deciding whether to go back to school or pursue other opportunities that have arisen since the bombing.

"He can do anything he wants really. But all he wants to do is walk. I think that's a good goal for now," she said. "Plus, we have the baby coming. That's going to be a big project. Like a lifetime project."

For this year's marathon, the couple plans to spend some time at the race, though Bauman admits to being apprehensive - not because he's worried it's not safe but because of his celebrity.

"I'm kind of scared about that," he said. "I don't want to be mobbed and hoisted up in a crowd."

6

THE TRIAL

The white van carrying Boston Marathon bombing suspect Dzhokhar Tsarnaev is escorted out of federal court following his arraignment in Boston. The 19-year-old Tsarnaev has been charged with using a weapon of mass destruction, and could face the death penalty, July 10, 2013. (AP Photo/Winslow Townson)

VICTIMS RELIVE HORROR OF MARATHON BOMBING AS TRIAL BEGINS
March 3, 2015
By Denise Lavoie

In the two years since twin bombs tore through crowds at the Boston Marathon finish line, the case against suspect Dzhokhar Tsarnaev has focused on arguments over where his trial should be held, who should sit on the jury and what evidence prosecutors should be allowed to use.

But starting Wednesday (March 4), a day after a jury was selected, the focus will shift dramatically from the legal process to the harsh reality of what happened that day: the explosions, the screams, the chaos and the blood.

Prosecutors are expected to present graphic images of the carnage caused by the bombs, including a surveillance video that authorities say shows Tsarnaev placing a backpack just feet from 8-year-old Martin Richard and his family. The boy died in the explosion.

The bombs set April 15, 2013, killed three people and injured more than 260. At least 16 people lost limbs.

"When people start streaming into that courthouse - many with missing limbs - and the prosecutors get up off their chairs and start talking about this again, people are going to relive the enormity and the awful nature of this," said Gerry Leone, a former state and federal prosecutor who led the prosecution of shoe bomber Richard Reid but is not involved in the Tsarnaev case.

Attorneys David Bruck, left, Judy Clarke, center, and Miriam Conrad, right, are the defense team for Boston Marathon bombing suspect Dzhokhar Tsarnaev, January 5, 2015. (AP Photos/File)

"It wouldn't surprise me to see the young boy's parents as the first witnesses. Oftentimes, in a homicide case, you humanize the victims right away, and you're brought right back to that day," Leone said.

A blast from the second bomb killed Martin and tore off his 7-year-old sister's left leg. Lingzi Lu, 23, a Boston University graduate student, was also killed by that blast. Krystal Campbell, a 29-year-old restaurant manager from Medford, was killed by the first bomb.

Authorities say Tsarnaev, then 19, and his older brother, Tamerlan, 26- ethnic Chechens who had lived in the former Soviet republic of Kyrgyzstan and the volatile Dagestan region of Russia - carried out the bombings to retaliate against the U.S. for wars in Iraq and Afghanistan. The brothers came to the U.S. with their parents and two sisters about a decade before the bombings.

Tamerlan Tsarnaev died following a shootout with police several days after the bombings. Dzhokhar Tsarnaev, now 21, faces 30 federal charges in the bombings and in the fatal shooting of a Massachusetts Institute of Technology police officer days later. Seventeen of the charges carry the possibility of the death penalty.

Some bombing survivors have said they plan to attend the trial; others say they have no desire to be there.

"It's not something I feel I need to do," said Jarrod Clowery, who suffered burns and shrapnel wounds. "I have closure in my life. I'm happy. I have a second chance at life, and I'm living it."

Clowery was watching the marathon with his friends, Paul and J.P. Norden, when the bombs exploded. The Nordens each lost a leg.

The Norden brothers also plan to stay away from the trial, but their mother, Liz, plans to be there every day. The trial is expected to last three to four months.

"It's important to me. I take it personally, what happened to my family," she said.

In addition to the video, prosecutors also plan to show jurors what they call a confession Tsarnaev scrawled inside the boat he was hiding in.

"The US Government is killing our innocent civilians but most of you already know that. ... I can't stand to see such evil go unpunished. We Muslims are one body, you hurt one you hurt us all," the note allegedly says.

"Stop killing our innocent people and we will stop."

Tsarnaev's lawyers have made it clear that they plan to depict Tamerlan Tsarnaev as the mastermind of the attack and a powerful force in his brother's life.

Legal analysts say portraying Tamerlan as a coercive influence will likely not be enough to win Dzhokhar an acquittal but could be a significant piece of the defense argument against the death penalty. After the guilt phase of the trial, the same jury will decide whether he should be sentenced to life in prison without parole or the death penalty.

The jury was chosen Tuesday after nearly two months of jury selection. The all-white panel consists of 10 women and eight men, including a self-employed house painter, an air traffic controller, a former emergency room nurse and an executive assistant at a law firm.

Tsarnaev may also get some help from his family. One of his sisters, Ailina Tsarnaeva, plans to attend at least part of the trial.

Liz Norden said she can't quite put her finger on why she feels such a strong need to be there.

"It's not about going and looking evil in the eye and seeing him. I realize I will never get the answers, but it's just very important to me that I go and see."

'IT WAS HIM': DEFENSE ADMITS TSARNAEV BOMBED BOSTON MARATHON
March 5, 2015
By Denise Lavoie

Members of the legal defense team for Boston Marathon bombing suspect Dzhokhar Tsarnaev, from left, Miriam Conrad, Judy Clarke and Timothy Watkins arrive at the federal courthouse in Boston, January 6, 2015. (AP Photo/Michael Dwyer)

The question, for all practical purposes, is no longer whether Dzhokhar Tsarnaev took part in the Boston Marathon bombing. It's whether he deserves to die for it.

In a blunt opening statement at the nation's biggest terrorism trial in nearly 20 years, Tsarnaev's own lawyer flatly told a jury that the 21-year-old former college student committed the crime.

"It WAS him," said defense attorney Judy Clarke, one of the nation's foremost death-penalty specialists.

But in a strategy aimed at saving Tsarnaev from a death sentence, she argued that he had fallen under the malevolent influence of his now-dead older brother, Tamerlan.

"The evidence will not establish and we will not argue that Tamerlan put a gun to Dzhokhar's head or that he forced him to join in the plan," Clarke said, "but you will hear evidence about the kind of influence that this older brother had."

Three people were killed and more than 260 hurt when two shrapnel-packed pressure-cooker bombs exploded near the finish line on April 15, 2013. Tsarnaev, then 19, was accused of carrying out the attacks with 26-year-old Tamerlan, who was killed in a shootout and getaway attempt days later.

Authorities contend the brothers - ethnic Chechens who arrived from Russia more than a decade ago - were driven by anger over U.S. wars in Muslim lands.

Federal prosecutors used their opening statements, along with heartbreaking testimony and grisly video, to sketch a picture of torn-off limbs, ghastly screams, pools of blood, and the smell of sulfur and burned hair in the streets of Boston. They painted Tsarnaev as a cold-blooded killer.

Tsarnaev planted a bomb designed to "tear people apart and create a bloody spectacle," then hung out with his college buddies as if he didn't have a care in the world, prosecutor William Weinreb said.

"He believed that he was a soldier in a holy war against Americans," Weinreb said. "He also believed that by winning that victory, he had taken a step toward reaching paradise."

Among the first witnesses for the prosecution were two women who lost legs in the attack, including Rebekah Gregory, who walked slowly to the stand on an artificial limb.

"I remember being thrown back, hoisted into the air," said Gregory, who had gone to watch the race with her 5-year-old son,

Noah. "My first instinct as a mother was, where in the world was my baby, where was my son?"

Boston Marathon bombing survivor Rebekah Gregory, right, and an unidentified woman arrive outside federal court in Boston, March 5, 2015. (AP Photo/Michael Dwyer)

She said she looked down at her leg: "My bones were literally laying next to me on the sidewalk and blood was everywhere." She saw other peoples' body parts all around her, and "at that point, I thought that was the day I would die."

"I could hear Noah, I don't know how, but I could hear my little boy. She said he was saying, 'Mommy, Mommy, Mommy,' over and over again."

"I said a prayer. I said, 'God, if this is it, take me, but let me know that Noah is OK.'"

She said someone finally picked up her son and put him down beside her. Breaking down in tears, she testified that as she looked for the boy, she saw a woman dead on the pavement.

Karen Rand McWatters, whose left leg had to be amputated, described how she watched her close friend Krystle Campbell, a 29-year-old restaurant manager, die on the pavement next to her.

"She very slowly said that her legs hurt, and we held hands, and shortly after that, her hand went limp in mine and she never spoke again after that," she said, choking back tears.

A shaggy-haired, goateed Tsarnaev slouched in his seat and showed little reaction as the case unfolded. The defense did not ask a single question of the four victims who testified Wednesday (March 4).

About two dozen victims who came to watch the case took up an entire side of the courtroom, listening somberly to details of the carnage. Several hung their heads and appeared to fight back tears.

Prosecutors also showed the jury a gruesome video of people lying in pools of blood. The footage was punctuated by screams, moans and the crying of a boy. The ground was strewn with ball bearings and chunks of metal, and smoke wafted over the victims.

The 10 women and eight men on the jury watched somberly. Several grimaced, especially at the sight of a gaping hole in a woman's leg.

In his opening statement, the prosecutor also described how 8-year-old Martin Richard stood on a metal barrier with other children so he could get a good view of the runners.

"The bomb tore large chunks of flesh out of Martin Richard," and he bled to death on the sidewalk as his mother looked on helplessly, Weinreb told the jury, with the boy's parents in the courtroom.

Because of a wealth of evidence against Tsarnaev - including a video of him leaving a backpack at the scene, and incriminating graffiti scrawled on the boat where he was captured - legal experts have said there is little chance of escaping conviction during the guilt-or-innocence phase of the trial.

Boston Marathon bombing survivors Heather Abbott, left, and Karen Rand, center, are escorted from federal court in Boston, after the first day of the federal death penalty trial, March 4, 2015. (AP Photo/Michael Dwyer)

Instead, they said, Tsarnaev's lawyers will concentrate on saving his life by arguing that Tamerlan was the driving force in the plot.

Clarke called the bombings "senseless, horribly misguided acts." But she asked the jurors to "hold your hearts and minds open" until the penalty phase, when the panel will decide whether Tsarnaev should be executed or get life in prison.

She held up two enlarged photos - one showing the two brothers years before the bombings, the other showing them carrying the backpacks containing the explosives - and asked the jury to contemplate: "What took Dzhokhar Tsarnaev from this ... to this?"

While the outcome of the guilt-or-innocence phase is now a foregone conclusion, it is not necessarily an empty exercise.

Robert Bloom, a Boston College law professor and former prosecutor, said the defense will use this phase to build the case that Tsarnaev was a follower, not a mastermind.

"They'll want to use every opportunity they can to show he was influenced by his brother," Bloom said. "Who bought the pressure cookers? Who bought the BBs? All of that."

Prosecutors, for their part, will use this portion of the trial to get across the horror of the attack and prime the jury to come back with a death sentence in the next stage, Bloom said.

Right up until the moment the jury filed into the courtroom, Tsarnaev's lawyers fought to have the trial moved out of Massachusetts, arguing that the emotional impact of the bombings ran too deep and too many people had personal connections to the case. But U.S. District Judge George O'Toole Jr. and a federal appeals court rejected the requests.

It is the most closely watched terrorism trial in the U.S. since the Oklahoma City bombing case in the mid-1990s.

Clarke has saved a string of high-profile clients from the death penalty, including Atlanta Olympics bomber Eric Rudolph; Unabomber Ted Kaczynski; and Jared Loughner, who shot and killed six people and gravely wounded then-Rep. Gabrielle Giffords in a 2011.

FATHER TELLS JURY ABOUT BOY'S DEATH
March 6, 2015
By Denise Lavoie

With Dzhokhar Tsarnaev seated at the defense table no more than 15 feet away Thursday (March 5), the father of an 8-year-old boy killed in the Boston Marathon bombing described the moment when he looked down at his son's pale, torn body and realized he wouldn't make it.

"I saw a little boy who had his body severely damaged by an explosion," Bill Richard told the jury, "and I just knew from what I saw that there was no chance, the color of his skin, and so on."

Martin Richard was one of three people killed in the bombing near the finish line of the race on April 15, 2013. The boy's younger sister, 6-year-old Jane, had a leg blown off, while their older brother, Henry, suffered minor injuries.

Their father, testifying at Tsarnaev's federal death penalty trial, spoke in a slow, halting voice but remained largely composed as he described the chaos and confusion.

He said he scooped Jane up in one arm and took Henry in the other and "tried to shield both of their eyes" from the carnage around them as he took them away.

Richard took the stand as federal prosecutors continued trying to drive home the consequences of the attack in such heartbreaking detail that Tsarnaev's lawyers objected - and were overruled.

A photograph of bombing victim Martin Richard, 8, is attached to a barricade at a makeshift memorial on the street not far from where two bombs exploded near the finish line of the Boston Marathon. Richard was among three people killed in the bombings at the finish line of the race, April 22, 2013. (AP Photo/Steven Senne)

Tsarnaev, 21, showed no reaction to the testimony and appeared to look straight ahead, not making eye contact with Richard, who sat off to the side in the witness box.

Some of the women on the jury appeared to wince at times during his testimony. Spectators in the courtroom could be heard crying quietly, including Rebekah Gregory, who lost a leg in the bombing.

As Richard testified, the jury watched a video of the father rushing to help his children and a grievously wounded Jane struggling to get up, only to fall down.

A prosecutor showed Richard a photo and circled a face - a young man in a white baseball cap worn backward- who could be seen just a few feet behind Jane and Martin as the youngsters stood on a metal barricade, watching the race. It was Tsarnaev, shortly before the two pressure-cooker bombs went off.

Richard said he himself suffered shrapnel injuries, burns on his legs and two perforated eardrums. His wife, Denise, was blinded in one eye and had other injuries.

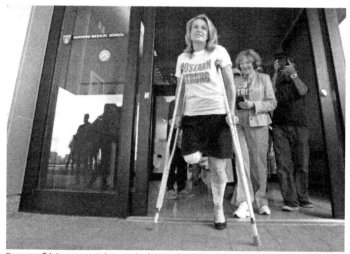

Roseann Sdoia uses crutches as she leaves Spaulding Rehabilitation Hospital in Boston. She was at the finish line on April 15, 2013, rooting for friends in the race, when the second bomb went off. Aside from her leg injury, she suffered hearing loss, May 14, 2013. (AP Photo/Charles Krupa)

Earlier Thursday (March 5), Roseann Sdoia testified that she saw two flashes of white light at her feet near the finish line, looked down, and for a split second thought to herself: I'm wearing strappy sandals.

She quickly realized she was looking at her foot dangling from her mangled leg.

"Someone came running over to me and told me I had to get out of there. I told them I couldn't get up. I didn't have a leg," a sobbing Sdoia told the jury.

She walked to the witness stand on an artificial leg, plainly visible below the hemline of her skirt.

Sdoia, who was at the race as a spectator, said she saw wounded people all around her, including someone covered with soot, dazed and "walking around like a zombie."

"It was almost like I was starring in a horror movie, as everybody else was around me," she said.

Prosecutors also showed the jury a grisly photo of her shredded leg.

Tsarnaev's lawyer has admitted the former college student took part in the bombings. But in a bid to save Tsarnaev from a death sentence, she argued that he was influenced by his older brother, Tamerlan, who was killed in a getaway attempt days after the bombing.

Also Thursday, Jeff Bauman - who lost both legs in the attack and was photographed being wheeled away that day in one of the most widely seen images of the tragedy - testified that he locked eyes with one of the bombers shortly before the twin blasts.

"He was alone. He wasn't watching the race," said Bauman, who walked slowly into court on two prosthetic legs. "I looked at him, and he just kind of looked down at me. I just thought it was odd."

Later, from his hospital bed, Bauman remembered the man's face clearly enough to give the FBI a description of someone authorities say turned out to be Tamerlan Tsarnaev.

Before testimony began Thursday, Tsarnaev's lawyers complained to the judge that the survivors' testimony from the previous day went into too much detail about the effect on their lives. They said that kind of testimony should be reserved for the punishment phase of the trial. U.S. District Judge George O'Toole Jr. said the testimony did not go too far.

POLICE DESCRIBE BATTLING MARATHON BOMBERS IN ESCAPE ATTEMPT
March 17, 2015
By Denise Lavoie

Three police officers on Monday (March 16) described an on-slaught of gunfire and bombs thrown during a violent confrontation with the Boston Marathon bombers days after the deadly attack and one suspect's furious escape in a stolen car that ended with him dragging his brother's body through the street.

The testimony by Watertown officers came hours after jurors in the federal death penalty trial of Dzhokhar Tsarnaev went to see the bullet-ridden boat he was found hiding in the evening of April 19, 2013.

An investigator examines a boat where officials apprehended a suspect in the Boston Marathon bombing in Watertown, Mass. Suspected bomber Dzhokhar Tsarnaev is hospitalized in serious condition with unspecified injuries after he was captured in an all-day manhunt the day before, April 20, 2013. (AP Photo/Julio Cortez)

Earlier that day, shortly after midnight, one officer spotted a carjacked Mercedes SUV on a quiet residential street. That set off a frenzied clash in which Dzhokhar and his older brother, Tamerlan, hurled explosives at police, including two pipe bombs and one pres-sure-cooker bomb similar to those used near the marathon finish line that killed 3 people and injured more than 260 others, the officers testified.

Joseph Reynolds, the first officer at the scene, said he "locked eyes" with the SUV driver, who was later identified as Tamerlan Tsarnaev. Reynolds said Tamerlan got out of the car and began firing at him.

"All I could see was muzzle flashes," he said. "I couldn't count it. It was nonstop."

The shots continued as other officers began to arrive, Reynolds said.

He saw a wick and a lighter and then watched as an object flew through the air, landed in the street and exploded, he said, shaking him to his knees.

"I could feel all the debris landing on top of me," he said.

Sgt. Jeffrey Pugliese said he cut through backyards to get closer to the bombers, and he eventually could see their feet illuminated by car headlights. He said he aimed at the ground near their feet in the hope that the bullets would ricochet into their ankles.

But Tamerlan saw him and came charging up the street, firing at him, said Pugliese, who fired back.

The two men came face to face, with only 6 to 8 feet separating them, Pugliese said. But Tamerlan had a problem with his pistol, the officer said.

"He kind of looked at his gun. He looked at me. We looked at each other," Pugliese said. "I think out of frustration, he threw his gun at me."

Pugliese said Tamerlan began to run away, but he tackled him. Tamerlan struggled as three officers tried to handcuff him, even though he was wounded and bleeding, Pugliese said.

That's when they saw the stolen car speeding toward them with Dzhokhar behind the wheel, Pugliese said.

The officer stepped out of the witness box to demonstrate how he tried to pull Tamerlan out of the way and how he rolled over to get himself out of the car's path.

"The black SUV, it was right in my face," he said. "I looked down, and I saw the front wheels were over Tamerlan."

Dzhokhar ran over his brother and dragged his body 25 to 30 feet, Pugliese said. He also struck a police car before he made his escape. Tamerlan Tsarnaev died of gunshot wounds and the injuries he received when being hit by the car.

After a massive manhunt and door-to-door search, Dzhokhar was found hiding in a boat parked in a backyard in Watertown.

A transit police officer at the shootout was gravely wounded and nearly bled to death. Dr. Heather Studley, an emergency room doctor, testified that Officer Richard Donohue was "essentially dead" when he arrived at the hospital.

Donahue had a gunshot wound to the groin and had lost nearly all the blood in his body on the street in Watertown, Studley said.

Studley said doctors brought Donohue back by giving him large infusions of blood quickly, installing a breathing tube and giving him epinephrine.

Earlier Monday, jurors went to see the boat, which was brought to a location in South Boston. The Associated Press was one of two news organizations and three courtroom sketch artists allowed to see the boat and provide pool coverage for the media.

The 18 jurors walked around the outside of the boat and peered inside, while Tsarnaev, flanked by three attorneys and U.S. marshals, watched impassively from a table about 50 feet away. As a defendant, Tsarnaev had a right to be present at the viewing.

The red and white boat is covered with more than 100 bullet holes marked individually with small pieces of white evidence tape. One of the boat's two front widows is shot out almost completely.

Wood from the power boat where Dzhokhar Tsarnaev was found hiding, etched with many words including "killing our people", is displayed in a conference room at the John Joseph Moakley United States Courthouse in Boston. The wooden pieces were presented to a jury in Tsarnaev's federal death penalty trial, March 17, 2015. (AP Photo/Charles Krupa)

Jurors took notes and then went two at a time onto a lift to look inside the vessel, which was on a trailer parked on a flatbed.

Inside the boat, they could see the note Tsarnaev wrote denouncing the U.S. for its wars in Muslim countries.

The note, written in pencil, is speckled with bullet holes and stained with blood, though the writing was barely visible.

Prosecutors said another portion of the note was carved by Tsarnaev into wood slats on the boat. It wasn't visible Monday but is expected to be shown to the jury later.

The judge ruled that the location of the boat could not be revealed to ensure the security of jurors and the defendant. The owner of the boat is expected to testify Tuesday.

Tsarnaev's lawyer admitted during opening statements that he participated in the bombings and the later crimes but said Tamerlan was the mastermind who recruited the then 19-year-old Dzhokhar to help him.

Prosecutors say Tsarnaev was a full and willing participant. Now 21, he faces the possibility of the death penalty if convicted.

The same jury that decides guilt will decide whether he receives life in prison or the death penalty.

BOSTON MARATHON BOMBER WANTED TO TERRORIZE US
April 7, 2015
By Denise Lavoie

As he planted a backpack containing a bomb near a group of children, Boston Marathon bomber Dzhokhar Tsarnaev made a coldblooded decision aimed at punishing America for its wars in Muslim countries, a federal prosecutor told the jury during closing arguments Monday (April 6) at Tsarnaev's death penalty trial.

"This was a cold, calculated terrorist act. This was intentional. It was bloodthirsty. It was to make a point," Aloke Chakravarty said. "It was to tell America that 'We will not be terrorized by you anymore. We will terrorize you.'"

Defense attorney Judy Clarke countered by arguing, as she did at the trial's outset, that Tsarnaev took part in the attack but did so under the malevolent influence of his now-dead older brother, Tamerlan. Clarke repeatedly referred to Dzhokhar Tsarnaev - then 19 - as a "kid" and a "teenager."

"If not for Tamerlan, it would not have happened," Clarke said.

The jury is expected to begin deliberating Tuesday morning in the case against Tsarnaev, 21, almost two years after the twin bombings near the finish line of the Boston Marathon killed three people and wounded more than 260.

If Tsarnaev is convicted - and that is considered a near certainty, given his lawyer's admission - the jury will then begin hearing evidence on whether he should get life in prison or a death sentence.

Prosecutors used their closing argument to remind the jury of the horror of that day, showing photographs and video of the carnage and chaos after the shrapnel-packed pressure-cooker bombs exploded. In one video, jurors could hear the agonizing screams of Krystle Campbell, a 29-year-old restaurant manager who bled to death on the sidewalk. Another woman and an 8-year-old boy were also killed.

Taking aim at the argument that Tsarnaev was led astray by his older brother, Chakravarty repeatedly referred to the Tsarnaevs as "a team" and "partners" in the attack.

Federal prosecutor William D. Weinreb arrives at federal court, Monday in Boston during the penalty phase of the federal trial of Dzhokhar Tsarnaev, who was convicted of the Boston Marathon bombings that killed three and injured 260 people, April 27, 2015. (AP Photo/Justin Saglio)

"That day, they felt they were soldiers. They were the mujahedeen, and they were bringing their battle to Boston," the prosecutor said.

As for the youngsters killed or maimed by the bomb that was in Dzhokhar's backpack, Chakravarty said: "These children weren't innocent to him. They were American. Of all the places that he could have placed the bomb, he placed it right there."

Tamerlan Tsarnaev, 26, died four days after the bombings after he was shot by police and run over by Dzhokhar during a getaway attempt. Dzhokhar was captured hiding in a dry-docked boat.

At the end of his closing argument, Chakravarty displayed photos of those killed in the bombings and the Massachusetts Institute of Technology police officer who was shot to death during the getaway attempt.

"They are no longer with us," Chakravarty said. "This is the result of the defendant's choice to be a terrorist, his choice to make a statement. These were choices that he was proud of."

Clarke struck a conciliatory tone in her closing argument, admitting the attack brought "tragedy, suffering and grief in dimensions that none of us could imagine were possible."

But in a strategy clearly aimed at saving Tsarnaev from the death penalty, Clarke said Tamerlan played a much more prominent role, buying bomb components, including pressure cookers, BBs and remote control parts. She said Tamerlan researched via computer how to build the bombs and planned the attack. And his fingerprints - but not Dzhokhar's - were found on pieces of the two bombs.

"We're not asking you to excuse the conduct," the defense attorney said, "but let's look at the varying roles."

TSARNAEV GUILTY ON ALL CHARGES
April 8, 2015
By Denise Lavoie

Dzhokhar Tsarnaev was convicted on all charges Wednesday (April 8) in the Boston Marathon bombing by a jury that will now decide whether the 21-year-old should be executed or shown mercy for what his lawyer says was a crime masterminded by his big brother.

The former college student stood with his hands folded, fidgeted and looked down at the defense table in federal court as he listened to the word "guilty" recited on all 30 counts against him, including conspiracy and deadly use of a weapon of mass destruction. Seventeen of those counts are punishable by death.

A sign with the photographs of Sean Collier, a Massachusetts Institute of Technology officer killed, and Richard Donohue, a Boston Police officer who was shot and critically wounded, is seen at a makeshift memorial on Boylston Street, near the finish line of the Boston Marathon, April 20, 2013. (AP Photo/Julio Cortez)

The verdict, reached after a day and a half of deliberations, was practically a foregone conclusion, given his lawyer's startling admission at the trial's outset that Tsarnaev carried out the terror attack with his now-dead older brother, Tamerlan.

The defense strategy is to try to save Tsarnaev's life in the up-coming penalty phase by arguing he fell under Tamerlan's evil influence.

The two shrapnel-packed pressure-cooker bombs that exploded near the finish line on April 15, 2013, killed three spectators and wounded more than 260 other people, turning the traditionally celebratory home stretch of the world-famous race into a scene of carnage and putting the city on edge for days.

Tsarnaev was found responsible not only for those deaths but for the killing of a Massachusetts Institute of Technology police officer who was gunned down days later during the brothers' getaway attempt.

"It's not a happy occasion, but it's something," said Karen Brassard, who suffered shrapnel wounds on her legs and attended the trial. "One more step behind us."

She said Tsarnaev appeared "arrogant" and uninterested during the trial, and she wasn't surprised when she saw no remorse on his face as the verdicts were read. She refused to say whether she believes he deserves the death penalty, but she rejected the defense argument that he was simply following his brother's lead.

"He was in college. He was a grown man who knew what the consequences would be," Brassard said. "I believe he was 'all in' with the brother."

Tsarnaev's lawyers left the courthouse without comment.

In the penalty phase, which could begin as early as Monday, the jury will hear evidence on whether he should get the death penalty or spend the rest of his life in prison.

Defense attorney Judy Clarke argued at trial that Tsarnaev was led astray by his radicalized brother, telling the jury: "If not for Tamerlan, it would not have happened." She repeatedly referred to Dzhokhar - then 19 - as a "kid" and a "teenager."

Prosecutors, however, portrayed the brothers - ethnic Chechens who moved to the United States from Russia more than a decade ago - as full partners in a brutal and coldblooded plan to punish the U.S. for its wars in Muslim countries. Jihadist writings, lectures and videos were found on both their computers, though the defense argued that Tamerlan downloaded the material and sent it to his brother.

Tamerlan, 26, died when he was shot by police and run over by his brother during a chaotic getaway attempt days after the bombing.

The government called 92 witnesses over 15 days, painting a hellish scene of torn-off limbs, blood-spattered pavement, ghastly screams and the smell of sulfur and burned hair.

Survivors gave heartbreaking testimony about losing legs in the blasts or watching people die. The father of 8-year-old Martin Richard described making the agonizing decision to leave his mortally wounded son so he could get help for his 6-year-old daughter, whose leg had been blown off.

In the courtroom Wednesday, Denise Richard, the boy's mother, wiped tears from her face after the verdict. The youngster's father, Bill Richard, embraced one of the prosecutors.

In Russia, Tsarnaev's father, Anzor Tsarnaev, told The Associated Press in recent days that he would have no comment.

The others killed in the bombing were Lingzi Lu, a 23-year-old Chinese graduate student at Boston University, and Krystle Campbell, a 29-year-old restaurant manager. MIT Officer Sean Collier was shot to death at close range days later.

Bombing victims from left, Martin Richard, 8, Krystle Campbell, 29, and Lu Lingzi, undated. (AP Photo/File)

In a statement, Collier's family welcomed the verdict and added: "The strength and bond that everyone has shown during these last two years proves that if these terrorists thought that they would somehow strike fear in the hearts of people, they monumentally failed."

Some of the most damning evidence at the trial included video showing Tsarnaev planting a backpack containing one of the bombs near where the 8-year-old boy was standing, and a confession scrawled inside the dry-docked boat where a wounded and bleeding Tsarnaev was captured days after the tragedy.

"Stop killing our innocent people and we will stop," he wrote.

Tsarnaev's lawyers barely cross-examined the government's witnesses and called just four people to the stand over less than two days, all in an effort to portray the older brother as the guiding force in the plot.

According to defense testimony, phone records showed Dzhokhar was at the University of Massachusetts-Dartmouth while his brother was buying bomb components, including pressure cookers and BBs. Tamerlan's computer showed search terms such as "detonator" and "transmitter and receiver," while Dzhokhar was largely spending time on Facebook and other social media sites. And Tamerlan's fingerprints, but not Dzhokhar's, were found on pieces of the two bombs.

Clarke is one of the nation's foremost death-penalty specialists and an expert at keeping her clients off death row. She saved the lives of Unabomber Ted Kaczynski and Susan Smith, the South Carolina woman who drowned her two children in a lake in 1994.

Tsarnaev's lawyers tried repeatedly to get the trial moved out of Boston because of the heavy publicity and the widespread trauma. But opposition to capital punishment is strong in Massachusetts, which abolished its state death penalty in 1984, and some polls have suggested a majority of Bostonians do not want to see Tsarnaev sentenced to die.

The 12-member jury must be unanimous for Tsarnaev to receive a death sentence; otherwise the penalty will be life behind bars.

During the penalty phase, Tsarnaev's lawyers will present so-called mitigating evidence to try to save his life. That could include evidence about his family, his relationship with his brother, and his childhood in the former Soviet republic of Kyrgyzstan and later in the volatile Dagestan region of Russia.

Prosecutors will present so-called aggravating factors in support of the death penalty, including the killing of a child and the targeting of the marathon because of the potential for maximum bloodshed.

Dan Collins, a former federal prosecutor who handled the case against a suspect in the 2008 terrorist attacks in Mumbai, India, said Massachusetts' history of opposition to capital punishment will have no bearing on the jury's decision about Tsarnaev's fate.

"When you ask people their opinion of the death penalty, there are a number who say it should only be reserved for the horrific cases," he said. "Here you have what is one of the most horrific acts of terrorism on U.S. soil in American history, so if you are going to reserve the death penalty for the worst of the worse, this is it."

Liz Norden, the mother of two sons who lost parts of their legs in the bombing, said death would be the appropriate punishment: "I don't understand how anyone could have done what he did."

7

SENTENCING

The John Joseph Moakley United States Courthouse is seen during the closing statements phase of the Dzhokhar Tsarnaev federal death penalty trial in Boston, May 13, 2015. (AP Photo/Stephan Savoia)

PHOTO, VIDEO OF TSARNAEV MAKING OBSCENE GESTURE RELEASED
April 22, 2015
By Denise Lavoie

Boston Marathon bomber Dzhokhar Tsarnaev peered into the security camera in the corner of his jail cell, fussed with his hair while looking in the reflective glass, flashed a two-digit salute like a teenager taking a selfie and then defiantly put up his middle finger.

A photo and video footage of the obscene gesture were released publicly Wednesday (April 22), a day after the photo caused a sensation when prosecutors showed it in court to the jury that will decide whether Tsarnaev lives or dies.

The images were taken by a video camera in Tsarnaev's cell three months after the April 2013 marathon bombings killed three people and injured more than 260. It was the day he was taken into court to be formally arraigned on 30 federal charges in the bombing and in the killing of a Massachusetts Institute of Technology police officer.

Prosecutors presented the photo, wedged between vibrant photos of the people Tsarnaev has been convicted of killing, during their opening statement, telling the jury it showed an "unconcerned, unrepentant and unchanged" Tsarnaev.

On Wednesday, Tsarnaev's lawyers tried to blunt the impact of the photo by showing video of Tsarnaev in his cell before and after.

The video shows Tsarnaev pacing around, fixing his hair and then climbing up on a bench and making the gestures. It shows an obvious injury to the side of his face where he was shot during a gun battle with police days after the bombings.

Defense lawyer Miriam Conrad emphasized Tsarnaev's young age when questioning Assistant U.S. Marshal Gary Oliveira about the video.

"How old was he at that time?" she asked.

Oliveira said he did not know.

"You don't know that he was 19 years old?" Conrad responded.

Testimony in the penalty phase of Tsarnaev's trial was to resume Thursday.

BOSTON MARATHON BOMBER CRIES AT FEDERAL DEATH PENALTY TRIAL
May 5, 2015
By Denise Lavoie

For the first time in court, Boston Marathon bomber Dzhokhar Tsarnaev dropped his blank, impassive demeanor and cried as his sobbing aunt briefly took the stand Monday (May 4) in his federal death penalty trial.

Tsarnaev, 21, wiped tears from his eyes quickly and fidgeted in his chair as his mother's sister sobbed uncontrollably. He had maintained an uninterested expression since his trial began in January.

The aunt, Patimat Suleimanova, cried as she sat down about 10 feet from Tsarnaev. The tears began falling before she began to testify, and she was only able to answer questions about her name, her year of birth and where she was born.

After a few minutes, Judge George O'Toole Jr. suggested that the defense call a different witness so she could compose herself. As she left the witness stand, Tsarnaev used a tissue to wipe his eyes and nose.

Five relatives - three cousins and two aunts - took the witness stand, though the aunt who broke down did not complete her testimony. As Tsarnaev was led out of the courtroom before the lunch recess, he blew a kiss at the other aunt, who also cried during her testimony. The relatives acknowledged they had not seen Tsarnaev since he was 8, when he moved to the U.S. with his family.

A relative of Dzhokhar Tsarnaev leaves federal court in Boston after testifying during the penalty phase in Tsarnaev's trial, May 4, 2015. (AP Photo/Steven Senne)

Tsarnaev, who had lived in the former Soviet republic of Kyrgyzstan and the Dagestan region of Russia, was convicted last month of 30 federal charges in the bombings, including 17 that carry the possibility of the death penalty. He moved to the U.S. in 2002 and committed the bombings, which killed three people and wounded 260 others, when he was 19.

Prosecutors say Tsarnaev and his radicalized older brother, Tamerlan, were equal partners in the bombing, and they have urged a jury to sentence Tsarnaev to death.

Tsarnaev's lawyers say Tamerlan, 26, was the mastermind of the attack and lured his brother into his plan. Tamerlan died days after the bombings following a shootout with police.

A cousin testified Monday that Dzhokhar was a kind and warm child, so gentle that he once cried while watching "The Lion King."

"I think that his kindness made everybody around him kind," Raisat Suleimanova said through a Russian interpreter.

Assistant U.S. Attorney William Weinreb pounced, asking her if she believes a deadly attack on innocent civilians can be considered kind. Tsarnaev's lawyer objected, and Suleimanova was not allowed to answer the question.

Shakhruzat Suleimanova, a sister of Dzhokhar's mother, Zubeidat, testified that Dzhokhar, Tamerlan and their two sisters were well-behaved as children.

"They were so good. They wouldn't hurt a fly," she said.

Suleimanova said the family was crushed when Zubeidat moved to the U.S. with her husband and children. Five or six years later, when Zubeidat returned to Russia for a visit, the family was shocked to see her sister, always a fashionable dresser, cloaked in black and wearing a Muslim headscarf. Tsarnaev's lawyers have argued that he was influenced by his brother and his mother, who had become radicalized in the years before the bombings.

"We were all shocked. We were all in pain. We were very scared," she said. "We had never had people like that in our family. We prayed, we fasted, but no people like that."

Another cousin, Nabisat Suleimanova, said Tsarnaev was loved by the entire family.

"He was an unusual child. He was wunderkind," she said.

She said he had a softening effect on an aunt who was very stern and strict with her own children but not with him.

Rosa Booth, a high school friend of Tsarnaev's, said she met him in a math class at Cambridge Rindge and Latin in 2011 and spent time with him and other friends.

"He had a sweetness about him, maybe a little shy," she said.

She said Tsarnaev, whom she described as "goofy," did not talk about politics or religion.

Prosecutors urged the judge last week to press Tsarnaev's lawyers to make sure his relatives testify soon because 16 FBI agents have been assigned, at great expense, to guard and protect them while they are in the U.S. The family members arrived in Boston on April 23.

Former classmate of Dzhokhar Tsarnaev, Rosa Booth, center, departs federal court in Boston after testifying during the penalty phase in Tsarnaev's trial, May 4, 2015. (AP Photo/Elise Amendola)

LAWYERS GIVE CLOSING ARGUMENTS IN MARATHON BOMBER'S TRIAL
May 14, 2015
By Denise Lavoie

Prosecutors and defense attorneys on Wednesday made their final appeals to the jury that will decide the fate of Dzhokhar Tsarnaev as jurors began deliberating whether the Boston Marathon bomber should get life in prison or the death penalty.

"The choice between these very serious alternatives is yours and yours alone to make," Judge George O'Toole Jr. told the panel.

Jurors got the case late in the day and deliberated for about 45 minutes before going home. They will return to the federal courthouse Thursday to resume their work.

The jury must be unanimous in its decision to impose the death penalty. If even a single member votes against death, Tsarnaev will get life in prison.

Prosecutor Steve Mellin said Tsarnaev wanted to cause his victims as much physical pain as possible to make a political statement.

"The bombs burned their skin, shattered their bones and ripped their flesh," Mellin said. The blasts "disfigured their bodies, twisted their limbs and punched gaping holes into their legs and torsos."

"Merely killing the person," he said, "isn't nearly as terrifying as shredding them apart."

Defense attorney Judy Clarke asked jurors to spare Tsarnaev's life, saying her client "is not the worst of the worst, and that's what the death penalty is reserved for."

She asked jurors to hold open their minds and try to understand how and why Tsarnaev became involved in the plot.

"We think that we have shown you that it's not only possible, but probable that Dzhokhar has potential for redemption," she said, adding that he was "genuinely sorry for what he's done."

The prosecutor showed a large photograph of 8-year-old Martin Richard, who was killed in the attack, and other children standing on a metal barricade near where Tsarnaev placed his bomb. Another photo showed bloodied victims on the sidewalk.

"This is what terrorism looks like," Mellin said.

Tsarnaev, he said, showed no regret after the bombings, calmly going to buy a half gallon of milk 20 minutes later.

"He acted like it was any other day. He was stress-free and remorse-free," Mellin said. "He didn't care because the death and misery was what he sought that day."

During the four-month trial, prosecutors portrayed Tsarnaev as a callous, unrepentant terrorist who carried out the deadly attack with his radicalized older brother, Tamerlan.

From the start, Tsarnaev's lawyers admitted he participated in the bombing, but they told the jury he was "a good kid" who was led astray by Tamerlan, who wanted to punish the U.S. for its actions in Muslim countries.

Clarke said Tsarnaev's parents favored his older brother and pinned their hopes on him, believing he would become an Olympic boxer. She showed photos of his father at boxing matches with Tamerlan, then asked "Where are the pictures of Dzhokhar? He was the invisible kid."

She noted the testimony of one witness who said the younger Tsarnaev followed his older sibling around "like a puppy."

The Tsarnaevs, who are ethnic Chechens, lived in the former Soviet republic of Kyrgyzstan and the volatile Dagestan region of Russia, near Chechnya, before moving to the U.S. about a decade before the bombings.

Death penalty opponent Sister Helen Prejean leaves federal court in Boston after testifying during the penalty phase in Dzhokhar Tsarnaev's trial, May 11, 2015. (AP Photo/Elise Amendola)

Tamerlan was a "jihadi wannabe" who returned to the U.S. angry and frustrated after an unsuccessful attempt to join Islamic extremists in Russia, Clarke said. Then he decided to find another way to wage jihad.

"If not for Tamerlan, this wouldn't have happened. Dzhokhar would never have done this, but for Tamerlan. The tragedy would never have occurred but for Tamerlan - none of it," Clarke said.

Mellin dismissed the contention that the older Tsarnaev somehow led his brother down the path to terrorism. "They were partners in crime and brothers in arms. Each had a role to play and each played it," he said.

Three people were killed and more than 260 injured when two bombs exploded near the marathon's finish line on April 15, 2013.

Tsarnaev, 21, was convicted by a federal jury last month of all 30 counts against him, including use of a weapon of mass destruction. The same jury must now decide his punishment.

Defense lawyers have said a life sentence would also help the families of his victims, who would not be subjected to the years of appeals and public attention that would almost certainly follow a sentence of death.

The defense showed the jury photos of the federal Supermax prison in Florence, Colorado, where Tsarnaev would probably be sent if he gets life. There, his lawyers said, he would be locked in his cell 23 hours a day - a solitary existence that would deny him the martyrdom he apparently sought.]

A sentence of life "reflects justice and mercy," Clarke said. Mercy "is never earned. It is bestowed, and the law allows you to choose justice and mercy."

She disputed prosecutors' characterization of Tsarnaev as unremorseful. She cited testimony of Sister Helen Prejean, who said Tsarnaev told her he was sorry about the pain and suffering victims endured.

"What unrepentant, unchanged, untouched jihadi is going to meet with a Catholic nun?" she said.

Mellin reminded jurors that some of them - before they were chosen for the jury - expressed a belief that a life sentence may be worse than death.

"This defendant does not want to die. You know that because he had many opportunities to die on the streets of Boston and Watertown. But unlike his brother, he made a different choice," Mellin said. "A death sentence is not giving him what he wants. It is giving him what he deserves."

JURY BEGINS DELIBERATING FATE
OF BOSTON MARATHON BOMBER
May 14, 2015
By Denise Lavoie

Just before a jury began deliberating the fate of Boston Marathon bomber Dzhokhar Tsarnaev, prosecutors reminded jurors of the pain and suffering caused by the bombing and said Tsarnaev deserves to die for what he did.

But Tsarnaev's lawyer said he was an "invisible" teenager in a dysfunctional family who was led astray by his older, radicalized brother and deserves a chance at redemption.

The federal jury of seven women and five men began deliberating late Wednesday after listening to powerful closing statements from prosecutors and Tsarnaev's lawyers. Jurors will return to U.S. District Court on Thursday to resume deliberations.

Prosecutor Steve Mellin told the jury that Tsarnaev is a callous "remorse-free" terrorist who bombed the marathon with his brother, Tamerlan, to make a political statement against the U.S. for its wars in Muslim countries.

Members of the media wait outside the John Joseph Moakley United States Courthouse during the closing statements phase of the Dzhokhar Tsarnaev federal death penalty trial, May 13, 2015. (AP Photo/Stephan Savoia)

Three people were killed and more than 260 were injured when two pressure-cooker bombers packed with shrapnel exploded near the marathon finish line on April 15, 2013.

Mellin said Tsarnaev wanted to cause his victims as much physical pain as possible.

"The bombs burned their skin, shattered their bones and ripped their flesh," Mellin said. The blasts "disfigured their bodies, twisted their limbs and punched gaping holes into their legs and torsos."

Defense attorney Judy Clarke asked jurors to spare Tsarnaev's life, saying her client "is not the worst of the worst, and that's what the death penalty is reserved for."

"We think that we have shown you that it's not only possible, but probable that Dzhokhar has potential for redemption," she said, adding that he was "genuinely sorry for what he's done."

The prosecutor showed a large photograph of 8-year-old Martin Richard, who was killed in the attack, and other children standing on a metal barricade. Tsarnaev placed his bomb just 3½ feet from the children. Another photo showed bloodied victims on the sidewalk.

"This is what terrorism looks like," Mellin said.

Tsarnaev, he said, showed no regret after the bombings, calmly going to buy a half gallon of milk 20 minutes later.

From the beginning of the trial, Tsarnaev's lawyers admitted he participated in the bombing, but told the jury he was "a good kid" who was led down the path to terrorism by Tamerlan.

Clarke said Tsarnaev's parents favored his older brother and pinned their hopes on him, believing he would become an Olympic boxer. She showed photos of his father at boxing matches with Tamerlan, and then asked, "Where are the pictures of Dzhokhar? He was the invisible kid."

The Tsarnaevs, who are ethnic Chechens, lived in the former Soviet republic of Kyrgyzstan and the volatile Dagestan region of Russia, near Chechnya, before moving to the U.S. about a decade before the bombings.

Tamerlan was a "jihadi wannabe" who returned to the U.S. angry and frustrated after an unsuccessful attempt to join Islamic extremists in Russia, Clarke said. Then he decided to find another way to wage jihad.

"If not for Tamerlan, this wouldn't have happened. Dzhokhar would never have done this, but for Tamerlan. The tragedy would never have occurred but for Tamerlan - none of it," Clarke said.

Mellin said the two brothers were "partners in crime and brothers in arms."

Tsarnaev, 21, was convicted by a federal jury last month of all 30 counts against him, including use of a weapon of mass destruction.

The defense showed the jury photos of the federal Supermax prison in Florence, Colorado, where Tsarnaev would probably be sent if he gets life. There, his lawyers said, he would be locked in his cell 23 hours a day - a solitary existence that would deny him the martyrdom he apparently sought.

A sentence of life "reflects justice and mercy," Clarke said.

Mellin reminded jurors that some of them - before they were chosen for the jury - expressed a belief that a life sentence may be worse than death.

"This defendant does not want to die. You know that because he had many opportunities to die on the streets of Boston and Watertown. But unlike his brother, he made a different choice," Mellin said.

"A death sentence is not giving him what he wants. It is giving him what he deserves."

TSARNAEV COULD BE FIRST TERRORIST EXECUTED IN US SINCE 9/11
May 16, 2015
By Denise Lavoie

The death sentence jurors imposed on Boston Marathon bomber Dzhokhar Tsarnaev sets the stage for what could be the nation's first execution of a terrorist in the post-9/11 era, though the case is likely to go through years of appeals.

In weighing the arguments for and against death, the jurors decided among other things that Tsarnaev showed a lack of remorse. And they emphatically rejected the defense's central argument - that he was led down the path to terrorism by his big brother.

The Friday decision - which came just over two years after the April 15, 2013, bombing that killed three people and wounded more than 260 - brought relief and grim satisfaction to many in Boston.

"We can breathe again," said Karen Brassard, who suffered shrapnel wounds on her legs.

Boston Marathon bombing volunteer first responder Carlos Arredondo holds a "Boston Strong" banner as he leaves the Moakley Federal court with his wife Melida after the verdict in the penalty phase of the trial of Boston Marathon bomber Dzhokhar Tsarnaev, May 15, 2015. (AP Photo/Charles Krupa)

A somber-looking Tsarnaev stood with his hands folded, his head slightly bowed, as he learned his fate, sealed after 14 hours of deliberations over three days. His lawyers left court without comment.

His father, Anzor Tsarnaev, reached by phone in the Russian region of Dagestan, let out a deep moan upon hearing the news and hung up.

The 12-member federal jury had to be unanimous for Tsarnaev to get the death penalty. Otherwise, the former college student would have automatically received life in prison with no chance of parole.

Tsarnaev was convicted last month of all 30 charges against him, including use of a weapon of mass destruction, for joining his now-dead brother, Tamerlan, in setting off two shrapnel-packed pressure-cooker bombs near the finish line of the race. Tsarnaev was also found guilty in the killing of an MIT police officer during the getaway.

Seventeen of the charges carried the possibility of a death sentence; ultimately, the jury gave him the death penalty on six of those counts.

The speed with which the jury reached a decision surprised some, given that the jurors had to fill out a detailed worksheet in which they tallied up the factors for and against the death penalty.

The jury agreed with the prosecution on 11 of the 12 aggravating factors cited, including the cruelty of the crime, the extent of the carnage, the killing of a child, and Tsarnaev's lack of remorse.

"Today the jury has spoken. Dzhokhar Tsarnaev will pay for his crimes with his life," said U.S. Attorney Carmen Ortiz.

With Friday's decision, community leaders and others talked of closure, of resilience, of the city's Boston Strong spirit.

Flowers rest at the finish line of the Boston Marathon after the verdict in the penalty phase of the trial of Marathon bomber Dzhokhar Tsarnaev, May 15, 2015. (AP Photo/Dwayne Desaulniers)

"Today, more than ever, we know that Boston is a city of hope, strength and resilience that can overcome any challenge," said Mayor Marty Walsh.

In weighing the mitigating factors, only three of the 12 jurors found Tsarnaev acted under the influence of his brother.

The defense argued that sending him to the high-security Supermax prison in Colorado for the rest of his life would be a sufficiently harsh punishment and would help the victims move on without having to read about years of death row appeals.

Massachusetts is a liberal, staunchly anti-death penalty state that hasn't executed anyone since 1947, and there were fears that a death sentence for Tsarnaev would only satisfy his desire for martyrdom.

But some argued that if capital punishment is to be reserved for "the worst of the worst," Tsarnaev qualifies.

Tsarnaev's chief lawyer, death penalty specialist Judy Clarke, admitted at the start of the trial that he participated in the bombings.

But Clarke argued that Dzhokhar was an impressionable 19-year-old led astray by his domineering 26-year-old brother, Tamerlan. The defense portrayed Tamerlan as the mastermind of the plot to punish the U.S. for its wars in Muslim countries.

Tamerlan died days after the bombing when he was shot by police and run over by Dzhokhar during a chaotic getaway attempt.

Prosecutors depicted Dzhokhar as an equal partner in the attack, saying he was so coldhearted he planted a bomb on the pavement behind a group of children, killing an 8-year-old boy.

Jurors also heard grisly and heartbreaking testimony from numerous bombing survivors who described seeing their legs blown off or watching someone next to them die.

Killed in the bombing were Lingzi Lu, a 23-year-old Boston University graduate student from China; Krystle Campbell, a 29-year-old restaurant manager; and 8-year-old Martin Richard, who had gone to watch the marathon with his family. Massachusetts Institute of Technology police Officer Sean Collier was gunned down in his cruiser days later. Seventeen people lost legs in the bombings.

Tsarnaev did not take the stand at his trial and showed a trace of emotion only once, when he cried while his Russian aunt was on the stand.

The only evidence of any remorse on his part came from the defense's final witness, Sister Helen Prejean, the Roman Catholic nun and death penalty opponent portrayed in the movie "Dead Man Walking." She quoted Tsarnaev as saying of the victims: "No one deserves to suffer like they did."

U.S. District Judge George O'Toole Jr. will formally impose the sentence at a later date during a hearing in which bombing victims and Tsarnaev himself will be given the opportunity to speak.

Tsarnaev probably will be sent to death row at the federal prison in Terre Haute, Indiana, where Oklahoma bomber Timothy McVeigh was put to death in 2001.

8

BOSTON STRONG

Sarah Vieira, 13, of Dartmouth, Mass., has "Boston Strong" written on her face during a baseball game between the Boston Red Sox and the Kansas City Royals in Boston, April 20, 2013. (AP Photo/Michael Dwyer)

DIAMOND, ORTIZ LIFT SPIRITS
April 20, 2013
By Jimmy Golen

A defiant David Ortiz stood on the Fenway Park infield and told the crowd to "stay strong," bringing a rousing cheer from Bostonians weary from a week of bombings, stay-at-home orders and a manhunt that locked down the city for a day.

Playing at home for the first time since two explosions at the Boston Marathon finish line killed three people and wounded more than 180 others, the Red Sox honored the victims and the survivors with a pregame ceremony and an emotional video of scenes from Monday's race.

"This past week, I don't think there's one human being who wasn't affected by what was going on down here," Ortiz said after the Red Sox beat the Kansas City Royals. "I was emotional, very angry about the whole situation. ... Everybody was hurting. I know it's going to take some time to heal up, but the one thing everybody's got to remember is that everybody supports each other."

Starting with a video, alternating between celebratory and somber and accompanied by Jeff Buckley's "Hallelujah," the tributes continued with a first-pitch ceremony that honored a first responder, a victim of the blast, and a marathon institution: Dick and Rick Hoyt, who have participated in the race for more than 20 years.

Then Ortiz took the microphone and, in what he later said was an unplanned outburst, let loose with an expletive that drew a huge cheer from the 35,152 who managed to make it through the beefed-up security and into their seats on time.

"This is our (expletive) city, and nobody is going to dictate our freedom," he said. "Stay strong."

Boston Red Sox's David Ortiz pumps his fist in front of an American flag and a line of Boston Marathon volunteers, background, after addressing the crowd before a baseball game between the Boston Red Sox and the Kansas City Royals in Boston, April 20, 2013. (AP Photo/Michael Dwyer)

Neil Diamond, who flew into town on his own and asked if he could sing, gave a live performance in the eighth inning of "Sweet

Caroline," the Fenway staple that has been adopted by opposing ballclubs to show their support for the city.

As Diamond, a New York native who wore a Red Sox cap, left the field, fans chanted "U.S.A.! U.S.A.!" In the bottom half of the inning, Daniel Nava hit a three-run homer to give the Red Sox the lead, and they held on to win 4-3.

"You give people hope," Ortiz said. "We wanted to let them know we're here for them."

Across town, the Bruins also returned to the ice after postponing their game against the Pittsburgh Penguins on Friday night, when a manhunt for the bombing suspects led to a "shelter-in-place" order that locked down the city. One suspect died and the other was captured, hiding in a dry-docked boat in a Watertown backyard.

Diamond singing "Sweet Caroline" in the eighth inning of a baseball game in Boston between the Boston Red Sox and the Kansas City Royals, playing at home for the first time since the Boston Marathon explosions, April 20, 2013. (AP Photo/Michael Dwyer, file)

"At least we could all breathe a little easier and sleep a little easier," coach Claude Julien said after the Bruins lost 3-2. "And now it's, hopefully, time to work ourselves into trying to get things back to normal again. But it will always leave a scar somewhere."

Penguins coach Dan Bylsma met with reporters before the game wearing a black T-shirt with words "Boston Strong" over his shirt and tie.

"I feel like we're playing with the Bruins today, not against them," Bylsma said before the game. "I know I share their pride yesterday in their city and their people and certainly their law enforcement yesterday. I'm certainly not a Bostonian, but I certainly share in that pride and hope to today with them as well."

The Bruins took the ice for their pregame warmup wearing baseball caps for the Boston and state police, along with one for the police in Watertown featuring the Bruins' "Spoked B" logo and the word "Strong" on the back.

Security was tight at both games, as it was when the Bruins made their emotional return after the bombing on Thursday night.

A SWAT team member with a German shepherd stood guard at the doorway to the tunnel leading to Royals dugout about 2 1/2 hours before game time. A man in military fatigues checked all of the players' lockers and the many cracks in the ceiling tiles with a flashlight.

Outside, fans milled around, waiting for the gates to open. Several of them were wearing Boston Marathon jackets dating back as long as a decade. Long lines of fans waited to be scanned by metal-detecting wands; many were still waiting to get in when the Red Sox and Royals lined up along the base-lines for the pregame ceremony.

With Boston Athletic Association volunteers in their yellow and blue jackets lined up in front of the Green Monster and police and public officials encircling the mound, ballpark organist Josh Kantor played The Star-Spangled Banner, with the crowd singing along. A giant U.S. flag was draped over the 37-foot-high Green Monster left-field wall, temporarily covering the "B Strong" logo newly painted in left-center field.

Pictures of the victims, including Massachusetts Institute of Technology police officer Sean Collier, were shown on the scoreboard, along with pictures from the marathon and the aftermath. Some of the biggest cheers were for the police who tracked down the suspects.

Gov. Deval Patrick and Boston Police Commissioner Ed Davis, along with other law enforcement officials and rank-and-file, circled the mound for the ceremonial first pitches from firefighter

Matt Patterson, who rushed to the site of the bombings; from Steven Byrne, who was injured in the explosions, and from Dick Hoyt, accompanied by his son Rick, who has cerebral palsy.

Ortiz, who had been on the disabled list all season, took the microphone and showed fans the specially designed uniforms saying "Boston" on the front instead of the "Red Sox" they have worn for decades. Both teams wore patches with the "B Strong" logo.

The Red Sox said their uniforms would be autographed and auctioned off to raise money for the One Fund Boston, the charity established to help the victims. The Boston Celtics, who opened their playoff series against the Knicks with a loss in New York on Saturday, said they would donate $100,000 to the charity, with another $100,000 to come from fundraisers.

The team said fans would be given the option to donate their refund from the canceled April 16 game against Indiana to One Fund Boston.

RUNNERS PLEAD FOR A SPOT IN MARATHON
April 20, 2013
By Jimmy Golen

"I need to run."

The messages started arriving just hours after the bombings, pleading for an entry into the 2014 Boston Marathon. For months the calls and emails continued, runners begging for an opportunity to cross the finish line on Boylston Street and convinced it would ease at least some of their grief.

"They'd say, 'I'm not a qualified runner; I don't think I ever will be. I train. I run. I could do it. But because of what happened last year, I need to run,'" Boston Athletic Association executive director Tom Grilk said last week.

"It might have been because they were present at the finish, or they knew somebody who was working or was affected. They might have been somebody who lives in Haverhill, Mass., and they were watching the race and it hit 'em hard. That was true for a lot of people.

"And we received some of these communications and we thought, 'What do we do?'"

The B.A.A. had already expanded this year's field to include more than 5,000 runners who were stranded on the course when the two explosions killed three and wounded 264 others. A few extra invitations were sprinkled among the first-responders and the victims, or their families; others went to charities and the towns along the route; some who said they were personally touched by the tragedy were already given bibs.

But organizers felt they might still be missing people, people who perhaps didn't think their trauma was worthy amid all the lost limbs and physical scars. So, in November, they announced that about 500 bibs would be available for those "personally and profoundly impacted by the events of April 15, 2013."

In 250-word essays submitted over the website, 1,199 would-be runners made their case. Almost 600 had the connection the B.A.A. was looking for.

"The anger, guilt and heartbreak I still feel today will never go away," wrote Kate Plourd, who was in the medical tent, dehydrated and vowing never to run Boston again, when she heard the announcements: "Explosions at the finish line. Casualties. Dismemberments. Prepare yourself to treat the victims."

"Running the 2014 Boston Marathon will help me heal my mind," she said in the essay that landed her bib No. 28115. "I'll push myself ... to finish the 2014 Boston Marathon in honor of those who won't ever give up, who I won't ever forget."

The last year in Boston has been punctuated with memorial services and other tributes, as well as fundraisers that have raised more than $60 million for the victims.

But for those who feel a connection to the Boston Marathon, that connection is most often felt through running.

And, when they decided they had to do something, they decided they had to run.

Dr. Alok Gupta, a trauma surgeon at Beth Israel Deaconess Medical Center, about 2 miles from the finish line, thought about treating so many leg injuries caused by the ground-level bombs and concluded that running the race would be "just really poetic."

"I decided that's what would be meaningful for me," said Gupta, who was a medical student in New York during the Sept. 11 attacks and has since studied disaster preparedness. "Running the Boston Marathon this year - not next year, not New York, not Chicago: Boston. I just thought it would be meaningful for me."

A competitive swimmer in high school, the now 37-year-old Gupta had no experience in distance running until he began to train for Monday's race. "We're on the second floor," he said in a recent interview at his office. "I took the elevator."

Googling "How long does it take to train for a marathon," Gupta got an answer of 18 weeks.

Patriots' Day was 18 ½ weeks away.

Pedestrians pass the spot where the first bomb detonated on Boylston Street near the finish line of the Boston Marathon, April 24, 2013. (AP Photo/Michael Dwyer)

He applied and received bib No. 35542.

Alan Hagyard ran Boston for the first time in 2012 and was back in the field last year, coming down Boylston when the first bomb went off about 30 feet away.

"The memories often bring tears to my eyes," he wrote in his application.

The explosion left him deaf in his left ear.

But he never considered sitting this one out.

"The next day, that night, I was ready to go again," said Hagyard, 67, of Hamden, Conn. "Partly to say, 'You can't stop us.'"

Having missed the qualifying time by 13 seconds, Hagyard wrote the B.A.A. to ask for a waiver. When organizers created the special invitation, he asked for a chance to rewrite the ending to last year's race.

"I want my current memory of Boston to be the perfect marathon," said Hagyard, bib No. 24812. "To run it again is to say, 'We're going to make it perfect this year, better than ever.'"

So many of those contacted for this story had the same request: Please don't make it about me.

The B.A.A. declined to make available those who read the applications, saying they wanted the attention to be on the runners. After sharing her story by telephone, finish line volunteer Adrienne Wald called back the next morning to express regret; after all, the victims had it much worse.

"It's weird to talk about being affected by the marathon," Plourd said. "No one I know was injured. A lot of us had really horrible experiences, but everyone walked away unscathed."

But the victims are "so inspiring," she said. "If people who have gone through this tragic experience can pull it together and be so strong, I figured I could, too."

Orthopedic surgeon Sue Griffith is raising money for Shriners Hospitals for Children in Philadelphia to supply prosthetics for children. She wrote that she was celebrating her finish last year "until I found out that the cannons I heard at the finish line were actually bombs."

Returning to work in Doylestown, Penn., she found her friend and running companion Amy O'Neill on her patient list with shrapnel deeply embedded in her calf.

They are returning to Boston together, Nos. 21321 and 21648.

"It's going to be a great event, and we're going to celebrate with the people of Boston," Griffith said in a telephone interview. "And that's

These are the people the B.A.A. was hoping to find, Grilk said, when it opened up the usually rigorous entry process for those who might qualify on an emotional level as well. Organizers heard from doctors and nurses and soldiers and victims and first-responders - the usual kind like police and firefighters, but also the ordinary individuals who rushed in to help.

Sarah Gasse, a nursing student who volunteered last year, said receiving her bib this way was itself an honor. Now 21, she wrote in her essay that her mother also ran the race when she was 21 and following her footsteps from Hopkinton to Copley Square had long been a goal.

"Because of my experience, it now holds an entirely new meaning for me," wrote Gasse, No. 28230. "Running the 2014 Boston Marathon would allow me to pay homage to those lost and injured that day, one more runner proving just how strong Boston truly is."

The submissions were raw with emotion, heavily introspective, often desperate, and yet unexpectedly hopeful.

Mike Chisholm, of Danvers, Mass., kisses his son Jacob, 3, before a baseball game between the Boston Red Sox and the Kansas City Royals in Boston, April 20, 2013. (AP Photo/Michael Dwyer)

"There are faces and images that I will never forget, and even writing about my experience now is proving more difficult than I had imagined," Gasse wrote. "Yet, despite the emotional trauma that ensued that day, I have a fire of passion in me that I have never known before. I am more confident than ever in my calling to work in health care."

One of about 20 UMass-Boston nursing students who volunteered last year to serve on a sweep team, Gasse was at the finish line with a wheelchair to scoop up exhausted runners.

"There's nothing like being at the finish line of the Boston Marathon," Wald, a nursing professor who had run the race five times, told her students. "You're going to be so inspired."

"I made them read articles about hypothermia, blisters, cramps. And instead they were carrying people with tourniquets around their legs and horrific injuries," Wald said on Tuesday, the anniversary of the attacks. "I was so worried that I had traumatized them all.

"I was worried they were going to change their majors. Instead they came into my office: 'I'm going to be an E.R. nurse now.' 'I'm going to work in trauma.' They saw role models that day coming out of the medical tent acting like the top pros that they are."

None of Wald's students was injured. But another UMass-Boston student, Krystle Campbell, was killed by one of the bombs.

Wald received bib No. 24741 and was hoping to run in Campbell's memory, but the injury that kept her from running last year could put her back on the sweep team with her students.

"Running would probably be the dumbest thing I ever do. But it's going to be really hard not to," she said. "It's an honor either way, to be part of this, to be able to contribute. If I can't run it, I am beyond happy, honored to help other people reach their goals."

The marathon can be a brutal sport, even more so when one considers that the 26.2 miles run on the day of the event are the culmination of a years-long process that, in Boston's case, begins with training for a qualifying race.

Runners looking for a reason to stop can always find one: the heat, the hills, the blisters, the cramps.

And now the threat of a terrorist attack, the memories of severed limbs, the ears ringing from the concussion of a bomb blast.

Yet for 118 years, runners have found a reason to make the trip to Boston. On Monday, more than 35,000 will leave Hopkinton to reclaim the euphoria of the finish line that was taken from them.

This year, three-time Boston champion Uta Pippig said, no one needs to ask them why.

"Running gives me freedom, and for a moment our freedom was restrained," she said this week. "That's what I believe is the reason we run together."

BOSTON MARATHON INVITES STOPPED RUNNERS BACK
May 16, 2013
By Jimmy Golen

Boston Marathon runners who were stopped on the course when bombs went off at the finish line will have a chance to come back and run again next year, race organizers said on Thursday.

Runners Linda DePoto, left, of Brighton, Mass., and Lauren Cain, of Brookline, Mass., stretch after crossing the finish line of the Boston Marathon in Boston. DePoto was one of the hundreds of runners who were denied the opportunity to finish the race on April 15 when officials halted the race because of the bombings, April 27, 2013. (AP Photo/Robert F. Bukaty)

One month and one day after the April 15 explosions that killed three people and wounded hundreds more, the Boston Athletic Association said that 5,633 people who were stopped on the second half of the course when the race was shut down at 2:50 p.m. will be allowed to register early for next year's race.

"The opportunity to run down Boylston Street and to cross the finish line amid thousands of spectators is a significant part of the entire Boston Marathon experience," B.A.A. executive director Tom Grilk said. "With the opportunity to return and participate in 2014, we look forward to inviting back these athletes."

The B.A.A. said runners who passed the halfway checkpoint at 13.1 miles but hadn't reached the finish line will get a code to register in August; regular registration is scheduled to begin in September. Runners will be required to pay the entry fee the amount hasn't been determined yet but they will not have to requalify by running another marathon in a given time.

Normal registration for the Boston Marathon requires a qualifying time from 3 hours 5 minutes for an 18- to 34-year-old man to 5:25 for an 80-year-old woman. The requirement forces most runners to spend a full year training for their qualifying and Boston runs and makes the race, for many, a one-time event.

The announcement was quickly praised on the B.A.A. Facebook page, where thousands of people many of them using the B.A.A. logo or other marathon-related photos for their profile picture "liked" the announcement. Hundreds posted comments vowing to return.

"I don't feel entitled to this in the least," wrote Maggie Lapan. "But thank you BAA."

The B.A.A. said it has contacted those affected, a group that includes 2,611 runners from Massachusetts and 726 from 47 countries. There are 2,983 women and 2,650 men, aged 18 to 82.

"Boston spectators are known for their impassioned support and unbridled enthusiasm, and they will give these returning athletes some of the loudest cheers at next year's race," Grilk said in the release, which added that no decision has been made on whether the 2014 field will expand to include an expected influx of runners who say they want to run next year to support the race and the city.

"We want to thank our participants for their patience as we continue to work through the details of arranging this accommodation for them," Grilk said. "And we ask for continued patience from the running community as we plan the 2014 Boston Marathon next April."

The B.A.A. has granted limited deferrals in the past, including one for European runners who couldn't get to town because of the Icelandic volcano eruption in 2010. Last year, with forecasts of dangerous heat, organizers allowed everyone a chance to defer their entry to this year's race; a few hundred took advantage of the offer.

IN SHOW OF DEFIANCE, 32,000 RUN
BOSTON MARATHON
April 21, 2014
By Jimmy Golen

Some ran to honor the dead and wounded. Others were out to prove something to the world about their sport, the city or their country. And some wanted to prove something to themselves.

With the names of the victims scrawled on their bodies or their race bibs, more than 32,000 people ran in the Boston Marathon on Monday in a powerful show of defiance a year after the deadly bombing.

Shalane Flanagan leads Buzunesh Deba, of Ethiopia, and Mare Dibaba, also from Ethiopia, and the elite pack past Wellesley College during the 118th Boston, April 21, 2014. (AP Photo/Mary Schwalm)

"We're marathon runners. We know how to endure," said
Dennis Murray, a 62-year-old health care administrator from Atlanta who finished just before the explosions last year and came
back to run again. "When they try to take our freedom and our de-
mocracy, we come back stronger."

The two pressure cooker bombs that went off near the end of
the 26.2-mile course last year killed three people and wounded
more than 260 in a spectacle of torn limbs, acrid smoke and broken
glass. But the city vowed to return even stronger, and the victory by
Meb Keflezighi - the first American in 31 years to win the men's race
- helped deliver on that promise.

On Twitter, President Barack Obama congratulated Keflezighi
and Shalane Flanagan, the top American finisher among the
women, "for making America proud!"

"All of today's runners showed the world the meaning of #Bos-
tonStrong," Obama wrote.

The race was held under extraordinary security, including 100
new surveillance cameras, more than 90 bomb-sniffing dogs and
officers posted on roofs.

As runners continued to drag themselves across the finish line
in the late afternoon, more than six hours into the race, state emergency officials reported no security threats other than some
unattended bags.

Kenya's Rita Jeptoo won the women's race in a course-record
2 hours, 18 minutes, 57 seconds, defending the title she won last
year but could not celebrate because of the tragedy.

Keflezighi, who did not run last year because of an injury, won
the main event this year in 2:08:37. A 38-year-old U.S. citizen who
emigrated from Eritrea as a boy, Keflezighi wrote the names of the
three dead on his bib along with that of the MIT police officer killed
during the manhunt.

As he was presented with the trophy and golden laurel wreath,
"The Star-Spangled Banner" echoed over Boylston Street, where the
explosions rang out a year ago.

"I came as a refugee, and the United States gave me hope,"
said Keflezighi, who was welcomed by fans chanting "U.S.A.!" "This
is probably the most meaningful victory for an American, because
of what happened last year."

At 2:49 p.m., the time of the first explosion, the crowd at the
finish line observed a moment of silence - then broke into some of

the loudest cheers of the day, with whooping, clapping and the clanging of cowbells.

This year's starting field of 32,408 included 600 people who were given special invitations for those who were "profoundly impacted" by the attacks, and almost 5,000 runners who were stopped on the course last year when the bombs went off.

"Today, when I got to that point, I said, 'I have to do some unfinished business,'" said runner Vicki Schmidt, 52, of Nashville. She added: "You can't hold us back. You can't get us down. Boston is magical. This is our place."

Some of the victims themselves returned for a ceremonial crossing of the finish line.

"It was hard. It was really hard," said Heather Abbott, who wore a "Boston Strong" sticker on the black prosthesis where her left leg used to be. "I was really nervous. I didn't want to fall. ... I'm just glad we made it."

Tatyana McFadden, who was 6 and sickly when she was adopted out of a Russian orphanage by an American, won the women's wheelchair race for the second straight year. Afterward, she spoke of Martin Richard, the 8-year-old boy who was the youngest of those killed in the explosions.

Spectators cheer along the route of the 118th Boston Marathon, April 21, 2014. (AP Photo/Steven Senne)

"I have a Russian heritage, but I am an American," McFadden said. "For today, not only was I running for Martin and his family, but all those other people that were affected by last year."

Dzhokhar Tsarnaev, 20, is awaiting trial in the attack and could get the death penalty. Prosecutors said he and his older brother - ethnic Chechens who came to the U.S. from Russia more than a decade ago - carried out the attack in retaliation for U.S. wars in Muslim lands.

Tamerlan Tsarnaev, 26, died in a shootout with police days after the bombings.

"It was a hard last year," Lee Ann Yanni, whose left leg was badly hurt in the bombing, said moments after crossing the finish line. "And we're just so much better and stronger."

DESISA WINS 119TH BOSTON MARATHON, ROTICH TAKES WOMEN'S RACE
April 21, 2015
By Jimmy Golen

Lelisa Desisa won his first Boston Marathon in 2013.

He didn't have much time to celebrate.

A few hours after Desisa broke the tape on Boylston Street, two bombs near the finish line turned what should be the pinnacle of any distance runner's career into an afterthought.

Desisa earned his second Boston Marathon title Monday (April 20), finishing in 2 hours, 9 minutes, 17 seconds to claim a golden olive wreath, the $150,000 first prize and a winner's medal to replace the one he donated to the city in memory of the victims.

And this one he plans to enjoy.

"This medal, I think, is for me," Desisa said.

Kenya's Caroline Rotich won the women's race, beating Mare Dibaba in a shoulder-to-shoulder sprint down Boylston Street to win by 4 seconds as the world's most prestigious marathon took a tentative step back toward normal.

Boston Athletic Association spokesman Jack Fleming interrupted the winner's news conference to place the trophy on the table next to Desisa and 2014 winner Meb Keflezighi and thank them both for helping the race heal.

"In 2013, Lelisa had won and we were sitting in these same chairs. And then soon after, and unfortunately, Lelisa did not get to have the kind of victory celebration that a champion of the Boston Marathon should have," Fleming said. "Lelisa, we want you to get your due today."

Desisa was in the leading pack for the entire race, pulling away to beat countryman Yemane Adhane Tsegay by 31 seconds in the first 1-2 finish for Ethiopia in the race's history. Kenya's Wilson Chebet was third, another 34 seconds back.

Dathan Ritzenhein of Rockford, Michigan, was the first American, in seventh. Keflezighi finished eighth a year after his victory - the first for an American man since 1983 - gave the city a tangible symbol of its comeback.

"I was crying on Boylston Street, because it was bringing up memories, good and bad," said Keflezighi, who wrote the names of the bombing victims on his race bib last year. "People were cheering like crazy, saying 'U-S-A!' I was chanting with them."

The 2004 Olympic silver medalist, who will turn 40 next month, was among the leaders until the 35-kilometer mark, when he took a drink of water that went down the wrong way. He had to stop five times to vomit.

Boston Marathon winner Lelisa Desisa, left, of Ethiopia, and women's division winner Caroline Rotich, of Kenya, pose with a trophy in Boston, April 20, 2015. (AP Photo/Charles Krupa)

As it did last year, the crowd encouraged him to go on. A few hundred feet from the finish, he sprinted to catch up to one of the female stragglers, grabbing her hand and crossing alongside her.

"It was an amazing opportunity for us to finish together," Keflezighi said. "Hopefully, it will be a memorable experience for both of us."

Two years after the explosions, "Boston Strong" was still ubiquitous - on shirts and signs, written in chalk on the street and shouted by spectators. But the crowds along the 26.2-mile course from Hopkinton to Copley Square were smaller than in 2014, no doubt thinned by the mid-40s temperatures, stiff wind and rain that was expected to pick up in the afternoon.

With many of the runners wearing long sleeves and gloves to fight off the cold, American Desiree Linden led for much of the women's race. But Linden fell off the pace in the final miles as Rotich and a pair of Ethiopians pulled away.

After Buzunesh Deba, last year's runner-up, fell behind at the final turn onto Boylston Street, Rotich and Dibaba ran together for the final quarter-mile, switching places before Rotich kicked into the lead for her first Boston title.

"I got to the last corner and I saw the finish line tape and I thought, 'This is it, I'm not going to let it go,'" said Rotich, who also collected $150,000 while giving Kenya its fifth straight women's champion. "I was like, 'No, not today.' And I kept going."

Rotich won in 2:24:55, with Deba in third. Linden finished fourth, and fellow U.S. Olympian Shalane Flanagan was ninth.

American Tatyana McFadden won her third straight women's wheelchair race, and Marcel Hug won his first men's title earlier Monday. Ernst Van Dyk, the most decorated Boston Marathon competitor in history, finished second in his attempt to win the race for an 11th time.

Security was visible but not intrusive for the second running since the bombings. State and local police, some riding bicycles and others on all-terrain vehicles, were supplemented by National Guard soldiers who walked alongside the road, applauding passing runners and occasionally reaching across the temporary fencing to high-five fans.

Officials were preparing for a crowd of 1 million spectators stretched along the route.

Like Desisa, they were also looking for something to celebrate.

"Last year was important to have a better ending than that day in 2013, and to support Boston," said Ramona Turner, who came from Winnipeg, Canada, to watch her husband run for the third year in a row. "This year, I'm here for the party."

TIMELINE OF EVENTS IN 2013 BOSTON MARATHON BOMBING
May 15, 2015
By The Associated Press

A timeline of events related to the Boston Marathon bombing, which killed three people and injured 260 others on April 15, 2013. A federal jury on Friday sentenced Dzhokhar Tsarnaev to death.

March 2011: Russian FSB intelligence security service gives FBI information that Tamerlan Tsarnaev, of Cambridge, Massachusetts, is a follower of radical Islam.

June 2011: FBI closes investigation after finding nothing to link Tamerlan Tsarnaev to terrorism.

Sept. 12, 2011: Bodies of three men are found in Waltham, Massachusetts, with their throats slit and marijuana sprinkled over them.

Late 2011: U.S. officials add the Tsarnaevs' mother to a federal terrorism database after Russia contacts CIA with concerns they were religious militants about to travel to Russia. She later says she has no links to terrorism.

January 2012: Tamerlan arrives in Russia, where he spends time in two predominantly Muslim provinces, Dagestan and Chechnya.

July 2012: Officials in Dagestan say Tamerlan applies for a new passport but never picks it up. Russian officials say they have him under surveillance but lose track of him after the death of a Canadian man who had joined an Islamic insurgency in the region.

July 17, 2012: Tamerlan returns to U.S.

November 2012: Islamic Society of Boston Cultural Center in Cambridge says Tamerlan has an outburst that interrupts a sermon about it being acceptable for Muslims to celebrate American holidays.

January 2013: Islamic Society says Tamerlan has a second outburst after a sermon that includes praise for the Rev. Martin Luther King Jr.

April 15, 2013: Bombs go off at the finish line of the Boston Marathon.

April 16, 2013: Federal agents say the bombs were made from pressure cookers packed with explosives, nails and other shrapnel, but they still don't know who detonated them or why.

April 17, 2013: President Barack Obama signs emergency declaration for Massachusetts and orders federal aid to supplement local response.

April 18, 2013: Investigators release photos and video of two suspects and ask for public's help identifying them. Later that night, Massachusetts Institute of Technology police officer Sean Collier is shot to death in his cruiser by Tamerlan and Dzhokhar Tsarnaev. They steal an SUV at gunpoint from a Cambridge gas station. The driver is held for about a half-hour, then released unharmed.

April 19, 2013: Tsarnaevs have an early morning gunbattle with authorities who have tracked them to Watertown. Tamerlan, who is run over by his younger brother, dies. Dzhokhar escapes, and at around 6 a.m., authorities tell residents of Boston and surrounding communities to stay indoors. All mass transit is shut down. That order is lifted around 6:30 p.m., just before authorities trace Dzhokhar to a Watertown backyard, where he is found hiding in a boat and taken into custody.

April 22, 2013: Dzhokhar Tsarnaev, injured in the shootout, is charged in his hospital room with using and conspiring to use a weapon of mass destruction.

April 30, 2013: Two friends of Dzhokhar's are charged with attempting to destroy evidence by disposing of a backpack and laptop computer taken from his room after they found he was a suspect in the bombing. Another is charged with lying to investigators.

May 9, 2013: Tamerlan Tsarnaev is secretly buried in Virginia after a weeklong search for a cemetery willing to take the body.

May 22, 2013: An FBI agent in Orlando, Florida, fatally shoots Ibragim Todashev, a friend of Tamerlan's, after he lunges at law enforcement officials questioning him about the Waltham killings. Officials say that before he died, he had agreed to give a statement about his involvement.

July 10, 2013: Dzhokhar Tsarnaev pleads not guilty to 30 federal charges.

July 23, 2013: Marc Fucarile is the last survivor of the bombings to leave the hospital.

Jan. 30, 2014: Prosecutors announce they will seek the death penalty against Dzhokhar.

April 15, 2014: Ceremonies and events mark the anniversary of the attacks.

April 21, 2014: The 2014 Boston Marathon features a field of 36,000 runners, 9,000 more than 2013 and the second-biggest field in history.

May 30, 2014: Khairullozhon Matanov, 23, of Quincy, is arrested on charges of obstructing the investigation by deleting information from his computer and lying to investigators.

June 18, 2014: Tsarnaev's lawyers file first of several requests to move the trial to Washington, D.C.

July 21, 2014: Azamat Tazhayakov, a college friend of Dzhokhar's, is convicted of obstruction of justice and conspiracy for agreeing with another friend to get rid of a backpack and disabled fireworks they took from his dorm room three days after the attack.

July 22, 2014: Stephen Silva, believed to have provided the gun used by the Tsarnaevs to kill Collier, is arrested on drug and weapons charges.

Aug. 22, 2014: Dias Kadyrbayev, 20, pleads guilty to impeding the investigation by removing incriminating evidence from Dzhokhar's dorm room.

Sept. 24, 2014: Judge grants delay and pushes start of trial to Jan. 5, 2015.

Oct. 28, 2014: Robel Phillipos, 21, of Cambridge, is convicted of lying to federal agents about being in Dzhokhar's room.

Nov. 25, 2014: Federal judge rejects a request from lawyers for Tsarnaev to order prosecutors to turn over evidence about his older brother's possible participation in the Waltham slayings.

Dec. 18, 2014: Tsarnaev appears in court for first time since his July 2013 arraignment.

Jan. 5, 2015: Jury selection begins in Tsarnaev's trial.

March 4, 2015: Tsarnaev's lead defense attorney, Judy Clarke, declares in opening statements: "It was him."

April 6, 2015: Prosecutors and defense present closing statements.

April 7, 2015: Jury begins deliberating verdicts.

April 8, 2015: Jury convicts Tsarnaev; will weigh possible death sentence in forthcoming penalty phase of trial.

April 15, 2015: Second anniversary of Boston marathon bomb-ings.

April 20, 2015: 119th running of the Boston Marathon.

April 21, 2015: Penalty phase of Tsarnaev's trial begins.

May 13, 2015: Prosecutors and defense make closing state-ments on sentence; jury begins deliberating.

May 15, 2015: Exactly 25 months after the attack, jury sen-tences Tsarnaev to death.

THE AP EMERGENCY RELIEF FUND

When Hurricane Katrina hit the Gulf Coast in 2005, many Associated Press staffers and their families were personally affected. AP employees rallied to help these colleagues by setting up the AP Emergency Relief Fund, which has since become a source of crucial assistance worldwide to AP staff and their families who have suffered damage or loss as a result of conflict or natural disasters.

Established as an independent 501(c)(3), the Fund provides a quick infusion of cash to help staff and their families rebuild homes, relocate and repair and replace damaged possessions.

The AP donates the net proceeds from AP Essentials, AP's company store, to the Fund.

HOW TO GIVE

In order to be ready to help the moment emergencies strike, the Fund relies on the generous and ongoing support of the extended AP community. Donations can be made any time at http://www.ap.org/relieffund and are tax deductible.

On behalf of the AP staffers and families who receive aid in times of crisis, the AP Emergency Relief Fund Directors and Officers thank you.

ALSO AVAILABLE FROM AP EDITIONS

**THE FALL OF
THE BERLIN WALL**

POPE FRANCIS

**CHRISTIANS
UNDER ATTACK**

**THE HUBBLE
SPACE TELESCOPE**

**THE COLLAPSE OF
THE SOVIET UNION**

MUHAMMAD ALI

MARIJUANA NATION

EBOLA

WARREN BUFFETT

CPSIA information can be obtained at www.ICGtesting.com
Printed in the USA
BVOW08s0655090615

403814BV00025B/253/P